Buffalo Chips

& Co.

To Dorothy!

Happy Trails!

Marilyn

MARILYN J. WILEY

Buffalo Chips

& Co.

Second Printing, 2011.

ISBN: 978-0-615-39315-15

Printed by InstantPublisher.com

Dedication

To Dolly and Dusty
Without whom the trip would not have happened

And

To the angels that went along for the ride

Foreword

Life! No one said it was going to be easy. But I never imagined it would be this *hard*. They say that whatever doesn't kill you makes you stronger. I suppose. Gold *is* refined by fire. But gold is an inanimate object and doesn't feel the heat. People do. I wrote this book for several reasons. First, it is because it was a unique adventure that should be shared. A wagon trip west! What could be more exciting? To those few thinking about doing the same thing, the experiences I share in this book will give you insight on such an endeavor. This story is also about surmounting personal obstacles as well as the natural ones.

The twelve-hundred mile walk was easy compared to the dreadful marriage that accompanied it. I wanted to separate the two subjects and focus only on the wagon trip. Then I realized the story I would be telling would be a lie. So I must apologize to you now, dear reader, that I did not choose a better person to accompany me on this trip. Had I done so, I would have had the time of my life. And this trip would have been more enjoyable for you, the reader, and me.

Another reason for this book is to encourage anyone that is on, or facing a difficult trail. That I believe is most of us. Few go through life without trials and tribulations. It is my hope that having been one who has already gone through the fire, my experience will encourage those of you still feeling the heat. No matter what trail you follow it *will* eventually come to an end. And it's not just the trail, but how we overcome the obstacles we encounter along the way.

Happy Trails!
Marilyn

The Trail West

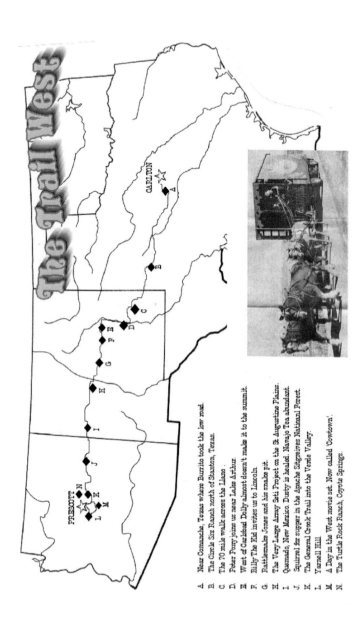

CARLTON

PRESCOTT

A. Near Comanche, Texas where Burrito took the low road.
B. The Circle Six Ranch north of Stanton, Texas.
C. The 70 mile walk across the llano.
D. Peter Pony joins us near Lake Arthur.
E. West of Carlsbad Dolly almost doesn't make it to the summit.
F. Billy The Kid invites us to Lincoln.
G. Rattlesnake Jones and his snake pit.
H. The Very Large Army Seti Project on the St. Augustine Plains.
I. Quemado, New Mexico. Dusty is healed. Navajo Tea abundant.
J. Squirrel for supper in the Apache Sitgreaves National Forest.
K. The General Crook Trail into the Verde Valley.
L. Yarnell Hill.
M. A Day in the West movie set. Now called 'Cowtown'.
N. The Turtle Rock Ranch. Coyote Springs.

TEXAS

It was nearly the end April, the spring of 1983. Our wagon was ready to roll. My family of four had prepared for the journey as much as we could. Our team of horses had been harnessed and were now hitched to the wagon. The designated driver would be me. The long leather driving lines in my hands felt oily and I pulled them back gently to make contact with the two mares fidgeting in front of me. When I felt the pressure of their mouths against the bits, I tapped the lines against their wide sorrel rumps and said, " Dusty! Dolly! Gid-up!" Thirty-five hundred pounds of horseflesh pushed forward into the leather collars, causing the trace chains to jerk tightly. The wooden double-trees creaked, and the reluctant weight of the wagon slowly rolled forward. The big red mares moved in unison down the long gravel drive towards the pavement of Texas Farm Road 2823. When we reached the corner, I swung them in a large arc to the right, facing west, towards our destination some 1200 miles away.

Buffalo Chips and Co. had just walked away from a tiny spot in the road known as Carlton, Texas. Had you watched this wagon-train-of-one as it departed you would first notice the big sorrel draft horses. Dusty was the mare on the left, the traffic side. Dolly, the older mare of the two, was on the right. Both were Belgian draft horses. Not giants as some draft horses are, but a more 'user friendly' size. Dolly, being the taller of the two, and Dusty making up for her shorter stature in sheer mass. Both were a brick red color, with palomino colored manes and tails. Dusty had long silky hair from her knees down, somewhat akin to a Clydesdale. She had a single white star in the middle of her forehead. Dolly had a blaze of white running the length of her face from her forelock down to her lips. The rest of her face was frosted with the white hairs that come with wisdom and age. Both mares were so tall that you could not see over their backs without standing on your toes. Their huge brown eyes showed excitement this morning. They were eager and ready to go. The harnesses they wore were old, dusty, and supple from too many years of use. In some places, the buckles were rusted, or broken, or even missing. Repair jobs were a quick bandage of twisted baling wire where a buckle *used* to be.

The wagon the mares were pulling was homemade. Just a rectangular shaped box built upon an old cotton trailer chassis. It was unpainted. Over ten feet tall from ground level to the top and eighteen feet from front to rear. The front had a porch across the breadth of it. Half of which was a seat, where I now sat. The other half covered an area where you could stand in front of the door into the wagon. The door itself was open on the top and closed on the bottom. It was a classic Dutch door design. Peeking out over the door were two little girls. They were my daughters. It was the start of a great adventure and they were excited. Helen was just six years old. She had flax colored hair tied back into pigtails. Her eyes were blue and she was tall for her age. She was thin but sturdy looking. Her younger sister Becky was only four. Her chestnut brown hair was tied back in a ponytail and her blue-green eyes sparkled like her sister's. In front of them sitting on the small porch was a smooth haired, honey color dog named Yeller. Almost Labrador looking but smaller and she had a bobbed tail. Her seven two-month-old puppies were in a large wire cage, bedded with straw, hanging beneath the wagon. They were quiet, uncertain of their situation, and curiously watched the eight legs of the horses walking in front of them.

At the back of the big wagon on the right-hand corner an Appaloosa mare was tied. She was buckskin colored with a large white rump that was sprinkled with buckskin spots. Towed behind the first wagon was a second wagon. This one was green with large red wooden wheels. It was a freight wagon. More of the style that one is accustomed to seeing with teams and pioneers. Its tongue attached it to the big box being pulled by the sorrel mares. Also secured to the back of the big wagon was a motorcycle. Tied to the right side in the center of the green wagon was a spotted sorrel and white tobiano stallion known as Cherokiowa Prince. He carried a saddle but no rider. Prince had the sweetest disposition of any stallion ever born. He was a delight to ride and the Cadillac model of the horse kingdom. I have yet to ride a smoother horse than the old spotted stud. He had great suspension and shocks. Following the rear of the green wagon was a sorrel yearling Quarter horse filly, and next to her, a small black and white spotted pony.

If one could have measured this entire rig from the tips of the draft mares' noses to the tail of the pony behind, they would have discovered that it was longer than a semi truck and trailer. Alongside the wagon, a fourth person rode my Quarter horse gelding Rocky. Rocky was an amazing horse, and truly deserves an entire book devoted to him. He was bay in color. Reddish brown with black legs and a black mane and tail. The only white on him was a large spot on his forehead. I bought him at the age of three from the Del Rio Springs Ranch in Paulden, Arizona. We were partners for the next thirty-two years. I had ridden him on ranch roundups in Arizona, at feedlots in the Texas Panhandle, and sale yards. He knew what it was to drag calves to a branding fire. He could get down and cut a cow. We had even done some endurance riding. Oh the stories he could tell! The fourth person riding Rocky was my former husband, and I will be referring to him as "Fourth Person."

We were embarking on a remarkable journey. Part of what made this trip so amazing was that we had *no* money. We were ready to go, and we had no money! I don't believe we had five dollars between us. That was nothing new. We seldom had any money. In order to get money; you had to have a *job*, which was a four-letter word to the Fourth Person riding Rocky. His more compassionate brother gave us thirty-six dollars that morning as we readied to leave. A person would have to be delusional to begin a trip like this with no more planning or finances than what we had. I don't think anyone who knew what we intended to do, walk all the way to Prescott, Arizona, from Carlton, Texas, thought we'd ever make it. What folly! But, as the old Chinese saying goes, "The journey of a thousand miles begins with the first step" is certainly true. And was obviously written by someone that walked everywhere they went. So into the West we walked.

That first day the spring air was light and filled with the scent of an unidentified fruit tree blooming in the distance. The green grass on either side of the roadway gave off a pleasant odor as the sun warmed it. This intoxicating fragrance made you want to inhale continually, and not take the time to exhale for loss of its sweetness. I had traveled this country road many times in a car but had never really seen it. Wild flowers dotted both sides of the roadway with blues, and yellows, and pinks. The bluebonnets Texas was famous for were in blossom. There were also scattered red spikes of Indian paintbrush, large yellow daisies trimmed in orange, and California poppies decorating both sides of this country road. Small creeks trickled through rusted steel culverts as we passed above them. Springtime in the Texas

Hill Country was beautiful. We were moving through it at a slow enough pace to experience it intimately. The road we were on was quiet, and seldom used. Occasionally a local farmer smiled and waved as he slowed and politely drove around us.

At midday I aimed the team onto a flat grassy area alongside the highway. The wagons easily rolled down the gentle slope, and as soon as the horses stopped all their heads disappeared into the high grass. After a quick lunch and a bucket of water for each of the horses, I picked up the lines and clucked, and the red mares pulled the wagons back up onto the pavement. The only livestock related mishap we had on the first day out was the lead rope that Prince was wearing had loosened, and had slipped below a wagon wheel. After stopping to make things right, we continued on our way. The other problem we encountered on the first day of travel was the metal rim on the rear wheel of the green freight wagon. It had loosened and continually had to be tightened to keep it from falling off. The wooden wheels were old and dry rotted. It would *never* make the trip. It hadn't even made it the first day out. A relative that arrived to check on us that evening pulled it back to the family farm we had just left. We were back to just the big wagon. Leaving the green wagon behind lightened the load considerably.

Camp the first night was about twelve miles from Carlton. There was a wide spot in the road with large areas of grass on both sides and a nearby creek. I parked the wagon on a flat spot, watered the horses, and then tied each out along the highway fence tethered to a fifty-foot rope. Each horse had his own stake out rope. The end would be tied to the bottom of a T- post on a swivel. On the opposite end a snap attached to each horse's halter. They could graze all night. By morning, there would be a mysterious line of crop circles, actually half-crop circles along the road, neatly mowed and fertilized.

Because we had so little money there would seldom be any sweet feeds, hay or grains for the horses. We could barely feed ourselves. We were poverty on wheels. I had to smile when a visitor stopped once and commented on how financially secure we must have been to be able to do this! And how he hoped someday he too could be so independently wealthy as to have a similar adventure. As I recall, dinner that night was a can of tamales split four ways. How did we come to be so destitute? The fault was mine. I made a bad decision. I accept the blame. I married poorly. No pun intended. The young man I had chosen to be with, for richer or poorer, had a job at the time, with a dream to someday own a ranch. The part I was not aware of was that he was going to steal the cows. You never really know someone until you marry them. And the longer I was married, the more I knew. His criminal tendencies made me ill. To avoid shame and ridicule, I just kept my mouth shut. As for the job he was fired eight weeks after our wedding. For the next fourteen years he seldom worked. A job here and there, a week, a day, but most of the time unemployed. He gave me something money couldn't buy- *Poverty*. An abundance of it. When the end finally came, it was not because of a lack of money. I had learned how to deal with that. It was his lack of character and morals. Until that day, because I was raised in a home where divorce was not an option, I rode it out. It was a rough ride.

We continually lived in a black hole of co-dependence with his parents. When he lost his job they allowed us to stay in their old dairy barn. From that we graduated to a tent, a garage floor, a fifty-year-old camp trailer, and then to his grandparents living room floor. For a while we lived in an overhead pickup camper sitting on the ground. One time for eight weeks we lived in a tipi. It never occurred to my then husband to find a job to provide for his wife and family. His parents did that. We ate all our meals with them. They handed him a few dollars every time he asked, which was almost daily. In return he would sit with his father, drink coffee and watch TV reruns of Andy Griffith, I Love Lucy, and the Beverly Hillbilly's all day long. This was their routine. It was this lifestyle that led me to flee, even if I had to walk, to a place far, far away.

Christmas Eve of 1982, my then husband presented me with the announcement that he had that day quit his job of six weeks as a highway trash lifter. Merry Christmas! With his last paycheck, he purchased Ninja stars, a Muslim head lobber, and a machete. If somewhere there were a society of irresponsible men, this man was their king.

I started making plans to ride my horse into the sunset. I would *have* to ride my horse. We had no car. Fourth Person's younger brother borrowed the last car we owned and it died in his hands. He drove it until the engine froze due to lack of oil. The whole family seemed to prefer changing engines instead of oil. A motorcycle was our last gasoline-powered vehicle. When I suggested to my spouse we return home to Arizona, via our horses, he decided it sounded like a lot of fun. I'm sure his thoughts were also thinking about how wonderful an excuse it would be to keep from finding and holding a job. He suggested we buy a cotton trailer, build a box on it for shelter, and buy a team. I had my two daughters to consider, and I knew it would be easier for them if we had a shelter of some kind. We had just received a settlement check from an insurance company for a dog bite my oldest daughter sustained. It was this small check that paid for the team and wagon project. Had we just purchased another old car, my then husband would never leave his parents. This was my escape plan to finally pull him off his mother's apron, and his father's government subsidized wallet. It worked! Two months later, we rolled.

That first evening on the trail, I pumped up the Coleman two burner stove and made bean burritos for dinner. Cooking on a Coleman stove is similar to cooking on a regular stove. If you've been camping, you may know what this is like. For you fortunate women who have an RV and have not experienced the delight of white gas cooking, let me educate you. First, you fill the red cylinder on the front of the stove with fuel known as white gas or Coleman fuel. It stinks. Don't spill it! That is not easily accomplished because the opening is about the size of a dime. After tightly replacing the cap, place the fuel can carefully in a place where it will remain upright, away from flame, clothing and children. On the side of the red cylinder you just filled is the plunger. You will need to twist it a bit to release it. Pull this out. Cover the tiny hole on the end of the plunger with your thumb as you depress the plunger. Pull plunger out, cover hole, push in. Pull plunger out, cover hole, push in. Repeat this process until the plunger gets difficult to depress. This pressurizes the canister and enhances your breast size at least on one side. Now you have primed the stove. Note: Remember to tie back your hair. Open one burner to the ON position. You should hear the hissing of fuel. Strike a match. When you see the flash and hear the BOOM, it's time to cook. An interesting side note of cooking on a Coleman stove is the never-ending black soot that accumulates on the bottoms of your pots and pans. This black soot is extremely difficult to clean. It has a tendency to contaminate everything within a city block around it. Towels, dishes, small children, pets, and your face. After you become familiar with the workings of your Coleman stove, you can also negotiate the Coleman lantern. It works on the same principles. Flammables, matches and explosions.

After dinner washing dishes was accomplished by boiling water in the coffeepot, and pouring it into a small rectangular tub, with dish soap and enough cool water to keep bare hands from scalding. You'll need to wash the pots last as they are coated in that wonderful soot from cooking. The pots are then left to air dry. If you try to dry them off, you will only succeed in turning your drying towel black with soot.

The inside of the wagon contained a wood L shaped kitchen area made of two by fours and plywood. Just a counter with an open shelf under it. The stove sat on the counter near the door. This was a safety feature. In the event the stove caught on fire it could be thrown out the adjacent door before it burned down the wagon. Thankfully, I only had to do that once. Further into the wagon was a piece of plywood about three feet wide and four feet long that served as a table. It was propped on one end by a two by four and the other end was nailed to the wall beneath the window. The far side of the table had a built-in bench of plywood for sitting. A wall the width of a full-sized mattress divided the front of the wagon from the back. Behind it was the sleeping area. There was a platform about hip high that held a mattress for the adults. About four feet above it was another same sized platform used for storage. It also served as a sleeping place for the girls during colder weather. Heat rises. The rest of the time, they slept in the space beneath the adults' platform. The inside of the wagon was almost eight feet tall, the same as the width. Including the porch it was eighteen feet long. I dubbed it the Whinney-Bago. The inside walls had thin wood grain paneling. The floor was plywood. There was no bathroom. The toilet consisted of a five-gallon bucket with a toilet seat attached. A plastic kitchen garbage bag was on the inside of the bucket. This slid under the bench at the table when not in use. There was no privacy.

We had no refrigerator. Instead we used one of those cheap, one dollar white Styrofoam boxes with a lid. It could hold a block of ice and a gallon of milk. We didn't need anything larger than that. We never had the money to buy food to fill it. We were truly living hand to mouth, day to day. There was no heat other than the Coleman stove. There was no cooling. The wagon had two slide up windows, one on either side, and we would leave the door open hoping for a breeze when it was hot. The windows were covered as we traveled. The two panels became a part of the side of the wagon. These panels came off easily when we stopped, for light and circulation.

A large rubber horse water tub sufficed for a bathtub for the girls. Baths happened for them once or twice a week depending on water availability. As for myself, I would bathe every night after dark. Working with hot sweaty horses, oily harness, and being outdoors in the elements always made me want a refreshing bath at the end of the day. It didn't take long for me to get bathing down to a science. Because it seemingly took hours to heat enough water on the Coleman stove at night for bathing, I washed out an empty one-gallon plastic milk container and filled it every morning. By keeping it on the wagon seat beside me in the sunshine, it warmed up enough to allow for a comfortable shower. Did you know you could bathe completely with a single gallon of warm water? Yes indeed! My shower stall was a three-step ladder we used to climb from the ground onto the porch of the wagon. It was made of two by fours and hooked onto the porch in such a way that it was stable and easily picked up to be tossed inside for travel. It was on this ladder I would stand, buck naked, after dark, with cars passing not far away, in order to bathe. Soap in hand and a gallon of sunshine warmed up water ready. Cautiously I would pour enough water from the jug onto each shoulder getting first one side, then the other of my body wet, being careful not to waste a drop. Then I would set the jug down and lather up. The rinse would be done with what water was left. It was important to have sufficient water to rinse the soap off with. Any place that was missed after the water ran out would have to be rinsed with water from the small storage tank on the porch, and it was always cold. After the soap and water ran off of me through the ladder and onto the ground, I grabbed my towel, and feeling refreshed, dried off and got ready for bed. This was my evening ritual. As for the Fourth Person, he didn't care much for bathing. Ever. Under any circumstances.

Our first goal on this leg of the journey was to arrive at the home of Rod and Liz Brinkman just outside of Comanche, Texas. It wasn't far in today's travel standards, only 35 or so miles, but it took us 3 days to get there with the wagon. The day before we arrived, a young man stopped at our evening camp, and purchased the young buckskin Appaloosa mare from us. Now we had some grocery money. That lucky horse missed out on the next twelve hundred miles of scenery. We would reinvest some of the money into another horse to resell down the road.

Figure 1. Painting the wagon in Comanche Texas.

The Brinkman's had a modest home on twenty acres. We stayed there for several days, at which time I painted the exterior of the wagon. The base coat was basically red. I painted two large oval shaped pictures, one on each side of the wagon. One side depicted a pair of wild stallions fighting, a stripe-backed buckskin sparring with Medicine Hat paint. The opposite side showed an Indian chasing a buffalo on his horse. Over the top of each oval painting were the words "Buffalo Chips and Co." I wanted it to look as much like an old Medicine Show wagon as possible. When I was a little girl, I had read a book about a pioneer family of four that rode in a wagon to California. The father was a magician. He called himself 'Mr. Mysterious', and the words "Mr. Mysterious and Co." were written on their wagon. It was a delightful story. At the time I read the book, I had no idea my future held a similar story. Deja vu. Fourth Person however, was not a magician. And for obvious reasons, I did not want "Cattle Rustler and Co." painted on the side of the wagon, so I chose something more appealing. The back of the wagon had a huge buffalo skull painted on it and I painted a smaller one that matched it above the driver's seat. The name Buffalo Chips seemed to work well with the paintings.

Across the front of the wagon, near the roof, were more stylized buffaloes against a gold colored background. I also painted lettering that stated, "Horses Bought and Sold, Western Art, Horse Shoeing, Wagon Rides, Photos, Sign Painting, Pony Rides, and Sheep Shearing". It was certainly colorful.

Rod and Liz Brinkman gave us a ride to the Brownwood horse auction that week where we spent some of the money from the sale of the buckskin Appaloosa mare. We purchased two unbroken mules to train and resell along the trip. The larger of the two we called Burrito. He was a solid black mule, full grown but young and wild as a deer. The smaller was a cute mini-mule we dubbed Taco. He was easier to handle, and gentled down quickly. After loading them into our friends' trailer, we hauled them back to our camp. Mules are a hybrid critter, the product of a male donkey or burro, and a female horse. They, being hybrid, are stronger, smarter, quicker, and tougher than either of their parents. It was said by one ol' mule skinner, that it's possible for a mean mule to bop you on the top of your head with his hind foot when you're standing right in front of his face looking at him, and so quick you'll never know what hit you!

Mules, being hybrid, also cannot reproduce. The wild black mule we had purchased needed to be castrated. This procedure would be similar to artificially inseminating a seven hundred-pound bobcat. Normally a veterinarian would have carefully injected a muscle relaxer into the artery in the neck, then administer another shot to put the patient to sleep. The animal would then wake up and the operation would be over. But that's not how Burrito lost his cahones. No vet here. Just the Fourth Person and his old pocket knife. I'll leave the details up to your imagination.

About the time the swelling was subsiding for the parties involved, we harnessed up the mares, and started down the road towards Brownwood. We were heading towards a secondary highway known as Highway 37. It is the main artery between towns of Comanche and Brownwood. The road leading from Brinkmans' onto Hwy 37 was dirt and barely one car wide. It led through the Texas Hill country, but remained fairly level and was a pleasant drive. The new mules were learning how to walk along with the whole procession but every so often would rebel and stop, or try to stop. But the wagon kept rolling, and they quickly learned to maintain the same speed - not too fast, and not too slow. Going too fast would cause them to attempt pulling the entire weight of the wagon with their head, and they quickly discovered that they did not have the strength to do so. And by stopping or slowing down, their necks would just stretch and they would drag along anyways. Being mules, they quickly found out how to walk along the path of least resistance. There were eyebolts drilled through and secured at the base of the wagon front and back on the right side. These were used as places to tie an extra horse, or mule, and Burrito the Black was tied to the rear eye bolt, away from my view.

At one place along this quiet dirt road, the trail narrowed down to cross a small bridge. The bridge was just wide enough for an eight-foot wide wagon with a black mule walking alongside, to pass. This wooden bridge looked sturdy enough for our heavy wagon and team to cross. It was made of thick planks and had sufficient bracing, but no guardrails; most likely because it was only five or six feet to the creek below. We took the high road and Burrito the Black took the low road. Too bad he was on a short leash. As the wagon rolled across, Burrito's body walked down into the creek bottom. However, his head stayed the same distance from the wagon. About the time his hind feet left the ground, Fourth Person noticed the situation and relayed the information. I stopped the wagon on the bridge. Burrito the Black was swinging from his halter like a giant black piñata off the right side of the bridge. Backing up was not an option. Due to its weight, this wagon only went one way - forward. But the same pocketknife that Burrito thought was going to kill him earlier that week saved his life by cutting the rope that held him. Burrito fell back with a thud, uninjured, and leapt across the creek to meet us on the other side. He was recaptured with a bucket of oats we kept back for horse bait in the event of such an escape. The way to a horses halter is through his stomach. Unharmed but humbled, Burrito the Black assumed his previous position by the wagon.

Later that day, the road turned to cross the railroad tracks that separated us from the main highway. Looking both directions I saw a distant light to my right coming down the tracks. It was over a half-mile away. Moving at four miles an hour we made the crossing in the same amount of time that it took the train to close the distance by half. My concern was how the horses and mules would react with the close proximity of a train. So instead of waiting I kept the mares going and they pulled the wagon up onto the crossing, then stopped. I had no idea why they stopped.

I had not asked them to. Perhaps they felt the earth rumbling and were curious. Perhaps they were afraid to cross the large metal tracks. All I knew was that this was no time for a rest stop. I could see the train plainly now, and I prayed "Please don't blow the whistle". I slapped the mares' butts with the lines, and they started again, walking down the other side, bringing the wagon and all aboard or tethered to it to safety. The highway was about 50 feet in front of us, and as we turned to the right onto it the trained passed. The train blew its horn and the engineer waved to me. The loud noise, the rattle and clanging had no effect on the team whatsoever. They never broke their stride and just kept clop clopping down the road. I was delighted with the knowledge that these mares that were taking us along for the ride would not frighten and try to bolt or run away. "Awesome" I thought, "If they were unconcerned about a train, nothing was going to rattle them!" I was delighted.

Whenever possible, we rolled along on the shoulder of the road. Sometimes it was paved, which made for smooth and quiet pulling, and sometimes it was dirt or gravel. I had to always be aware of highway signs, guardrails, and other highway markers, and make allowance for the horses and mules walking alongside, so they wouldn't get squished, or wrapped around a sign. Water was always a concern, "Where to find it, and it *had* to be found". The small water tank we had on board was only good for one evening's requirement of water. I watched for windmills, creeks, ponds, irrigation ditches, sprinklers, puddles, cow tanks, and water spigots. During the trip, we obtained water from all of these.

For the people on board we had a seventeen-gallon, Government Issue military surplus Gerry can. It's what we drank and cooked out of and when necessary, gave the horses. A single draft horse could drink twenty-five to thirty gallons of water every twenty-four hours. We had two draft mares, so we needed at least sixty gallons a day for them alone. Add the others to that, and although they drank fewer gallons, water was the biggest priority on the trip, and we needed a lot of it. I do believe the real pioneers lost a lot of livestock on the trails west. We didn't have anyone supplying us with a support vehicle and were not part of a wagon train, but instead depended on the numerous towns, farms, and people along the way to provide us with the water we needed.

Figure 2. A lunch break near Brownwood, Texas.

The first hill of any size loomed in front of us as we left the town of Brownwood, heading for the small community of Bangs. Up until then, any slopes we had traveled were only slightly uphill or downhill. The mares had to seriously work to get up this steeper incline. If you had been in a car, you probably wouldn't have even noticed it. This was the first time the entire weight of the wagon compared to the weight of the team was realized. The mares weighed about thirty five hundred pounds. The wagon was closer to four thousand. Fortunately for Dusty and Dolly it was a short distance to the top.

Imagine yourself standing on a street, with a little red Radio Flyer wagon. If you put enough sacks of feed in that wagon to equal your own weight, you could give the wagon a good tug, and roll it down a level street with not much difficulty. However, pulling it up a hill would wear you out in a hurry. The steeper the hill the harder you would have to pull. And going down a steep slope, its weight would tend to shove you down. It would be a struggle on a really steep decline to keep it from running over you, or pushing you off balance and down. For this trip when extra horse-power was needed the person on the saddle horse would put a lariat loop around the front of the wagon tongue that was protruding out between the team. Then dally around the saddle horn with the other end of the lariat. Riding out in front of the team, the extra horse could help pull the wagon when the hills were long or steep.

The big red wagon had a friction brake on it. It was a simple contraption made from a steel pipe that made contact with both rear tires when engaged by a rope. When pulled upon by the driver it was capable of slowing things down, but was by no means able to stop the wagon on a steep road. By my engaging the wagon brake, I could keep most of the weight of the wagon off the mares when going down a slope. This made going downhill easier on the horses. There was another emergency brake available that I only employed once on the entire trip. His name is Burrito the Black. I will describe how that worked when we get to that portion of the trip.

The next small towns we encountered were Bangs and Santa Ana. Between the two we were stopped and interviewed by a reporter for one of the local papers. He took some pictures and wrote a short article. When you're bright red, ten feet tall, and surrounded by moving objects, people take notice. It's a wonder we didn't cause any wrecks along the way due to people looking at us. Once an older gentleman drove up and spoke to the Fourth Person. He wanted to know if we were heading for a harvest. When told we were just "going down the road", the old man commented, "Oh. Bums, huh?" With age comes wisdom.

We slipped into a daily routine before long. Each morning we were on the road by nine a.m. Not that we slept in, but just because of the time it took to water, harness, and saddle all the stock. Helen and Becky would have their bowl of cold cereal. Hot meals were saved for the evenings. Lunch was just a sandwich. This was our normal fare as long as we had money to buy groceries. Sometimes, as we drove away from a town, we had not made any money and therefore could not buy any food. Dinners could be sparse.

Figure 3. One of the author's drawings sold along the trail.

I, being an artist, had brought along prints of drawings I had done to sell for five dollars to anyone who wanted one. I also sold stationery note cards with envelopes that were made from some of my drawings. My oil paints were with me and if we were stopped for a day to let the horses' rest, I would paint pictures of draft horses onto flat, plain white dishes. I also had my leather working tools along, and made buckles to sell. The rattlesnake skins ones were the most popular. When we found a fat rattlesnake along the way it was skinned and turned into several buckles. Three, four or five, depending on the length. We only ate one once. It wasn't the flavor that turned me off, or the numerous bones, it was the way the serpent crawled around in the skillet while it cooked! Some things we just weren't meant to eat. I also made wallets from scraps of leftover cowhide, and sometimes hand carved some western style belts. It was common at our roadside camps for folks to stop to visit. At these times, I displayed my drawings, paintings and other items, in hope that an item or two could be sold for the cash we needed to sustain us. We also had a Polaroid camera for taking instant pictures of visitors' children, which we sat on the pony, dressed in a fringed buckskin shirt. Pony rides were a dollar. A photo was five. Yes sir, we had our own entrepreneurship enterprise on wheels. On rare occasions we sold one of the extra horses. But most of our income was from artwork or pony rides and photos.

Traveling alongside the highway at an average of four miles per hour, it was hard not to notice the unlimited cast off aluminum cans alongside the road. It seemed to make sense to me for the Fourth Person to start picking them up as he rode over the top of them. We could then turn them in for much needed cash along the way. He fashioned himself a long stick with a nail sticking out one end, efficient enough to poke a can while still riding the horse. All he had to do was reach over with his stick and poke it. His horse never even had to slow down. The Fourth Person did try to get the horse to flatten them with its foot before they were stabbed, but the horse just couldn't get the hang of it. The large black plastic garbage bag filled to the brim in a day or two. In the evening, Becky and Helen would make a game of smashing the cans flat. At the next town the cans were cashed in for eighteen dollars and change. That was the extent of our recycling attempt. Fourth Person never picked up another can. He seemed to think it was too much work, not enough money for his labor, and interfered with whatever else he was doing.

Ballinger, Texas had a large city park banking a river that a passerby told us about. I pointed the mares that direction. As with most campsites, we didn't ask if we could, we just did. I stopped Dolly and Dusty at the far end of the park, close to the river end of it and we camped for two days to let all the horses rest and eat the tall green grass that grew around the park perimeter. People coming to the park with their families sometimes came over and bought note cards and let the kids ride the pony. Whenever a few dollars were made it meant there would be groceries for our next day's journey west.

While we were at the Ballinger Park, a TV cameraman and reporter from Abilene showed up and put us on the evening news. He portrayed us as an unusual American family seeking adventure! Modern day pioneers heading west! When in fact, we were broke, homeless, unemployed and near starving. We could have won the award for being America's Most Dysfunctional Family.

The narrow two-lane road down into the Ballinger Park was steep. Getting down there wasn't a problem. Climbing out would be. Our first attempt was a near disaster. The mares made it half way up the hill and were stopped by the weight of the wagon. I pulled on the brake but it wouldn't hold, and the wagon started rolling backward, dragging the team with it. The two horses tied at the back were forced into maneuvering themselves to stay out of the way of the backward rolling wagon. I jackknifed the mares to the left, and allowed the wagon to roll crosswise in the road. Then I swung the mares to the right, back towards the bottom, went down and circled, then lined up once more for the climb. This time ol' Rocky and Fourth Person tied onto the wagon tongue. We hit the bottom of the hill at a good trot and with Rocky pulling for all he was worth, the mares slipping on the pavement and struggling to push their weight forward, we barely made it to where the road leveled out. What a relief! I was careful not to allow ourselves to get in a predicament like that again. That was the steepest short climb we encountered on the whole trip.

Figure 4. One of the many photos taken on the pony.

We stopped in the center of town and made a trip to the neighborhood grocery store. The next town we'd come to was Bronte. It was two days away. Not knowing if Bronte had a market I tried to stretch our few dollars enough to sustain us in the event of having to make it to the town beyond that. Ice, tortillas, cheese, canned refried beans, milk, cereal, butter and bread. Lunchmeat if we could afford it, but that was a luxury. Fresh fruits and vegetables were expensive and we had no way to keep them cold. And finally, some crackerjacks for the girls.

One morning as we were on this leg of the journey, a kind passerby stopped and handed us several fresh catfish fillets from his daily fishing trip. I had no way to cook them except in a black cast iron skillet on the Coleman stove. Battered with a little dry flour, and cooked in a pat of margarine, they were delicious. Much more so than the rattle-snake. Thank you again Sir, whoever you were, for your thoughtfulness. The Bible has a verse in it that says "Be not forgetful to entertain strangers: for thereby some have entertained angels unawares." I think the good Lord was providing for us like the birds of the field. Perhaps this man was an angel in disguise. Quien sabe? He was the first of many we met. There would be others further down the trail.

We stayed on Highway 156 all the way through Bronte and on to Robert Lee. There we drove down to a grassy area at the base of the Ev Spence reservoir. I wasn't too keen about camping at the base of an earthen dam holding back trillions of gallons of water. But the entire town of Robert Lee was situated below the dam also and had been there for a long time. I prayed it would hold for a day or two while the horses tanked up on the deep, lush grass at its base. We were in west Texas now. The air was dryer, the vegetation was thinning out, the trees were shorter, and the grass along the highways was only deep and green where the rain had puddled. Finding suitable campsites was getting more difficult for want of feed for the horses.

At a truck stop on the way out of town a semi hauling whole corn had pulled away and left a pile of it right in our path! It had seeped out through a crack in the bed of the truck. We stopped and scooped it up with our hands. We filled buckets and gave all the horses several mouthfuls of it while they stood, still harnessed to the wagon. The scene reminded me of the movie Ten Commandments, when Moses raided the temple granaries. The horses chomped away at it like hungry children eating a candy bar. There was enough to last the horses several days. Another angel had crossed our path. It was like manna from heaven.

That evening's camp at Robert Lee surprised us with a special treat. We were invited to use the shower and bath

Figure 5. The view from the driver's seat.

facilities of a bunkhouse a mile or so away. Perhaps these kind folks had been downwind of the Fourth Person, but whatever the reason it was delightful to shower with un-limited water. *Hot* water. Helen and Becky were happy to not have to bathe in the rubber horse tub. With a few drops of liquid dish soap they splashed in a tub full of bubbles. As I remember back, I do believe that even the Fourth Per-son took a shower that evening. And that didn't happen very often. There was a washer and dryer available in the same cabin so I washed all of our dirty clothes. Washing clothes while on the wagon trip was only done when water was plentiful. It was more important to keep the horses alive than keep all the laundry clean. Fourth Person did his part by wearing the same clothes for at least a week before changing. Dirty laundry was kept in a plastic laundry bas-ket awaiting abundant water. Sometimes I would use the pony for a pack animal and lead him through the streets of a town to the local Laundromat. Our clothing tied in pil-lowcases hanging from his saddle. I often wanted to invent a five gallon bucket that could be filled with dirty clothes, water and soap, then seal the lid and place it atop a moving mule or pony's pack saddle. By the end of the day, the walking animal would slosh the clothing, soap, and water, making for perfectly washed clothes. The sun would even heat the water! All I would have to do is rinse. Perhaps I could market it as the 'May Nag.'

Meanwhile, back in reality, washing of our laundry was more often than not, done the old-fashioned way. By hand using a scrub board. The rubber horse tub would be filled with soap and water from a creek, windmill, or hose. I would heat water on the Coleman stove to bring the temperature up to lukewarm. Hand scrubbing would begin. As clothing was washed, it was put in a pile next to the tub, awaiting a fresh tub of clean water for rinsing. After rinsing, it was hand wrung and hung out to dry on the highway fence. Those little barbs on the wire work better than clothespins. Larger items were draped over the top wire. Smaller items, like underwear, could be snagged on a single barb. Yes, wash day was always special. It added a certain color to the scenery along the busy highways we traveled, as America drove by, looking at our undergarments flapping in the breeze.

From Robert Lee, we headed north to Colorado City, a trip of forty-four miles and over three days travel time. Along this road we met a gentleman by the name of Jerry Bob Taylor. He was in charge of a Baptist Church Camp further west, just six miles north of the Texas town of Stanton. He invited us to come stay at the camp and rest the horses. He had a string of dude horses coming in for the summer, and could use a hand with them. This would mean staying in one place for awhile. As it turned out we would need to. Dusty was in trouble.

Since the town of Bronte, Dusty had picked up an annoying habit of tossing her head after being hitched to the wagon. Every third or fourth step she took, her head would fly upwards, as if being bitten by a fly. Her behavior stopped when we unhooked for the night. Then the next day it would begin again. Horses sometimes pick up nasty habits like this because of the bit. Either rebelling against it due to constant pressure from a rider, or because the bit was loose and was banging against a sore tooth. I had light hands, and seldom pulled tightly on the lines. In fact, most of the time, the lines were loose with no mouth contact at all. Just an occasional correction if the horses swayed too far to the left or right. The mares knew where their place was on the highway. They were so steady that Becky and Helen could drive them. I had no idea why Dusty was reacting this way, but it became apparent after we arrived at the church camp a week or two later.

Between the church camp and us were the towns of Colorado City and Big Spring. At the former we turned west and followed the main highway I-20 on a frontage road. We were considered pedestrians by the law and legally not allowed on an interstate. Technically however, we could move onto an interstate when there was no frontage road available to us. This we did to cross large bridges when a side road was not available. Thankfully the local authorities never happened by at those short intervals when this was necessary. I would often put the horses into a slow trot and use that blazing speed to get us off of the highway as soon as possible. Had flashing red lights appeared I would not have been able to produce a driver's license or proof of insurance because I had none. Neither is required when you're driving a horse drawn vehicle. But I had no desire to enlighten anyone wearing a badge of that fact.

Between Colorado City and the next small town of Coahoma the frontage road crossed over a creek filled with fresh clear water. Stopping the wagon just off the pavement, I grabbed a five-gallon bucket and walked back to the bridge. There was a pool of water about 2 feet deep below the small bridge we had just crossed. I tied the end of one of the horses strong stake out ropes to the bucket handle and threw the bucket over and down into the creek below. The water was twenty feet down. The bucket hit with a splat, then turned and started to sink. When it was about half filled, I started hauling the water up. Hand over hand, pulling the rope up. When the bucket reached the top, the water was emptied into a wider bucket the horses could drink out of. It would take upwards to fifteen minutes or more to slake the thirst of all the horses this way. The old saying of "You can lead a horse to water, but you can't make him drink" is not true. The horse they used for that example wasn't one of these. Our horses would drink every time.

Big Spring Texas was the largest town we had passed through thus far. We drove along the frontage road and stopped for lunch in the dirt parking lot of an old livestock auction yard. A young man riding a nice Paint stallion that looked a lot like Prince rode up to greet us. As we talked we came to find out it was one of Prince's sons. A horse named Rick O Shay Shawn. The rider told us about a campsite with lots of water and grass not far away. We let the horses rest and took a lunch break while we visited with Rick O Shay's owner.

Whenever we took a short break, if grass was available, we tied the peripheral horses out to graze. It was always important to tie them to an immovable object. Something they would be connected to when you came back. Usually a sturdy fence post, a tree, a wagon, an anvil or some such thing. A piece of rusted corrugated galvanized steel sheeting lying on the ground should not be ones first choice. However, that day for some reason only known to the Fourth Person, Taco the mule was secured to such a thing, the end of his rope poked through a hole in the steel. Taco the mini mule weighed around four hundred fifty pounds. The corrugated steel weighed about ten pounds. As Taco grazed out to the end of his line, the sheeting started to follow him. And the faster he went, the faster the sheeting followed. When the sheeting reached the end of the grass and hit the gravel, it started to scrape and rattle, and Taco went into hyper speed. The parking lot was nearly empty, and that was a good thing. Taco was doing laps with a flying sheet of sharp metal behind him, sometimes airborne, or sliding sideways as he made the corners. In the midst of his panic, Taco sought refuge back in the herd, and headed back our way. Having a half-broke mule running towards you at break neck speed, with a large sharp object bouncing along behind him will certainly focus your attention. The girls were safe up in the wagon. Rick O Shay and his owner made themselves scarce. The other horses all tucked themselves as far away from the racket as possible as Taco sped by. The only thing that stopped him was a half-rotted broken post sticking up out of the ground. It was just high enough to catch the rope and hang up the metal, and strong enough to stop a wild eyed mini-mule. There were no injuries and that was a miracle.

Later that evening we camped at the city park, close to the famous Big Spring for which the town is named. The spring itself was a circular swampland area with a large clear pool in the center. Rick O Shay's owner was correct. Grass and water were plentiful. A black topped narrow road made the park accessible to visitors. The mowed area around the wetland was dotted with campsites. I stopped the mares in a remote area and we tied out the horses for the night. Curious onlookers stopped to visit, and we sold a few pony rides to visiting children. One particular couple with a young teenage son in tow came up to the wagon and introduced themselves. It seemed our reputation had preceded us. Relatives had tracked us down! A cousin, her husband and their son Dusty. They lived in Big Spring and had heard about our adventure through the family grapevine. We spent the evening visiting with them, and made arrangements for their son Dusty to ride with us when we left the church camp several weeks later. That was our next destination. It would take us two days to walk to the Baptist church camp located six miles north of Stanton. When we arrived at the Circle Six Ranch it would be for an extended stay while we helped them with their dude string.

The next morning found us driving once again along the frontage road of Hwy 20. The horses had gorged themselves on green grass and were somewhat refreshed. Dusty was still behaving strangely, tossing her head almost continually as she walked.

Traveling at a blazing four miles an hour allows you to notice everything you pass. At this stretch of road, it was interesting to listen to the sounds of the vehicles on the highway next to us. Something about the pavement made the tires of the cars along the interstate abreast of us almost musical. As a vehicle would hit a certain spot along this road, their tires would react with the pavement in such a way as to produce a brrrr or humming sound. Becky and Helen had dubbed it the 'Singing Road'. Some vehicles would have a high pitch tone, others low and grumbly. When several went through this area in a group, their individual sounds produced a chaotic melody. A bass background music to our own clip clop, clip clop of the horses.

Thus far on our adventure, the weather had been for the most part very mild. We had not experienced any of the nasty spring weather west Texas is known for except for one quick rain near Robert Lee. That particular day a small storm slowly materialized on the horizon. A cold breeze hit us first, then blowing dirt and finally the rain. Lightning split the air and cracked with a frightening boom! I pulled the mares to a stop.

Shelter was nowhere in sight. No overpasses, no trees. Just flat land Texas as far as I could see. The wind picked up and there was not so much as a hill to buffet it. So we just stood at the side of the road, faces into the wind and rain. Dusty and Dolly tucked their tails, lowered their heads and stood rock still. Then the hail began. Marble size pellets bounced off the backs of the team. I watched helplessly as the pebbles of ice beat Dolly and Dusty. There was nothing that could be done. To their credit, they did not bolt and run. They fidgeted back and forth in their harnesses, wishing they could turn their tails to the storm, but were locked in their places with leather and chains. The thick harness softened the blow in spots, but most of their bodies were exposed. The other horses and mules used the tall wagon as a break against the unwelcome hail. The closer ones pushed themselves against it to get as far away from the stinging ice as possible. I had left the plywood seat and stood in the doorway to escape the downpour, still holding the lines to the team. The wagon had proved a worthy shelter from the elements. Helen and Becky were safe and secure from the weather. The storm subsided in about fifteen minutes and we drove on. Puddles of rainwater laced with hail formed in some low spots of the pavement. I stopped the wagon to let the big horses drop their heads and drink. After the team drank, I moved them forward so the others tied to the wagon could each reach the temporary rain pool. This water was painfully delivered, but refreshing.

The day we left Big Spring started warm and windless. At the west Texas town of Stanton I pointed the mares north. The church camp was an hour and a half down the road. That's a trip of only six miles to anyone else not riding on a horse drawn wagon. The sky started turning red and the wind picked up. I'm sure all the horses smelled the coming storm before I did. The obedient mares walked on, Dusty still tossing her head. The other horses and two mules kept a steady pace. Helen was enjoying riding the black and white pinto pony along the fence line that separated the two-lane road from the farmland that surrounded us. Becky sat alongside me on the wagon seat. The Fourth Person rode alongside the wagon more often than not. He enjoyed being the spokesperson for our adventure. Being

on a horse allowed him to stop and talk with folks while I
kept the wagon rolling. Sometimes, much to his delight,
they handed him money. Finally, in the distance I could see
the overhead gate of the Circle Six Ranch. Also to the
north, I could see the lower sky had turned a dark reddish
brown across the *entire* horizon. A west Texas dust storm
was bearing down on us! We were going north, and it was
coming south. The sun was slowly being blotted out by the
dirt in the air.

Helen tied her pony back to the wagon and jumped up
on the porch. She and Becky went back inside the wagon
and closed the bottom half of the Dutch door. This desert
dust storm was a terrifying sight. A wall of dust and dirt
thousands of feet high was approaching rapidly. The blasts
of wind were getting fierce. It flashed through my mind
that our ten-foot tall, top heavy wagon could be toppled by
this oncoming wind. The wind gusts of thirty to thirty-five
miles per hour was now blowing hard sand into Dusty and
Dolly's faces. They were walking directly into it. Debris
from the farmlands that flanked the road shot at us. Tumbleweeds, feed sacks, loose branches hung up momentarily
on the horses legs, then bounced off to continue down the
road. The wall of dirt had moved closer. I asked Dolly and
Dusty to pick up speed and trot into the oncoming storm.
Their eyes would be nearly closed now, if not shut tightly
to avoid the stinging sand. They obeyed my directions and
trotted blindly into the storm. As it started to spit rain. I
swung the mares to the right, still trotting, and passed under
the Circle Six Ranch gate entrance. The wall of dirt was
nearly on top of us now. Dusty and Dolly were happy to be
turned away from the brunt of the storm. But we still
needed shelter, and we needed it *now*.

Just past the main house on the right was a tall shop
building. The wind was buffeting the side of the wagon and
it was swaying dangerously. I trotted the mares up as close
to the shop as possible, leaving only a couple of feet be-

tween the wagon and the building. The building was long enough to give protection to the entire length of the wagon and its animals. As I pulled the mares to a stop, a wall of dirt blasted over the shop and covered us. The sky went dark and we found ourselves in a fog of swirling sand and dirt. Jerry Bob and his family were there immediately to help get the horses secured and put up for the night. I thanked God for holding back the storm just long enough for us to find shelter. We had arrived at the Circle Six.

The next morning as I was brushing the dust and dirt off of Dusty, I noticed a large swelling on the top of her neck where the collar rests, hidden beneath her thick flaxen colored mane. The swelled area was about the size of my fist. Dusty tossed her head as I gently squeezed the lump to inspect it. A stream of pus came shooting out of the top several inches into the air. Dusty had fistula. Now I understood why she had been tossing her head. I washed her wound with peroxide and applied some Furazone ointment. Fistulas are caused by two hard surfaces bruising the tissue between. Horses with protruding backbones and not enough saddle pads are prone to it. When a poorly fitting saddle rubs against the backbone it destroys the skin and tissue beneath. An empty saddle does not cause the condition. The weight of the rider on the wrong saddle is the culprit. In Dusty's case, it was not the weight of her collar that caused it, but the weight of the wagon tongue. In his infinite wisdom, the Fourth Person had used a heavy steel pipe instead of a normal wooden wagon tongue for the big wagon. Because Dolly was the taller of the two, Dusty bore the weight of the tongue on her neck. All 60 pounds of it pressing the collar down into her neck. The constant rubbing of the past two hundred plus miles had done its damage. It would be a long time healing. It was good to be stopped for awhile. I hoped it would be time enough for Dusty to heal. Each morning and evening we would clean Dusty's wound with peroxide and ointment. Because there was no place for the infection to drain, it was no better when we left than when we arrived. Dusty had a hole in the top of her thick neck about the size of a golf ball. I would stick my finger into it to clear the pus each day. The hole held it like a hollow egg. It would take a long time to heal.

Jerry Bob Taylor was a generous host. In exchange for our labors with the dude string, we had access to shower facilities in one of the bunkhouses, beds if we wanted them, a laundry area, and meals provided for our horses and us. There was also a swimming pool which Helen and Becky enjoyed. And a game room that kept the Fourth Person up nearly all night every night playing Pac Man. Breakfast, lunch and dinner were provided in the camp cafeteria. What a blessing not to have to cook on the old Coleman stove!

We all enjoyed the variety of foods available. It was a feast compared to our regular fare of beans and tortillas. They had fresh melon slices and fruit. Apples, corn on the cob, and fresh lettuce for salads. We were being treated as honored guests. Sometimes I would help in the kitchen, cleaning and washing the piles of dirty dishes. Jerry Bob also hired me to repaint the signs around the entire ranch, which kept me busy for weeks.

Each week brought new groups of children to the camp. Hundreds of them! Helen and Becky had plenty of children to play with. The campers enjoyed arts and crafts, Bible stories, swimming, horseback riding, and evening stories around the campfire. Jerry Bob dressed up like a mountain man to entertain the children, and tell them about Jesus. He wore authentic leather clothing complete with fringes all around, and a coonskin cap. He had a real black powder rifle. Jerry Bob was tall, and carried himself like Charlton Heston. The children were mesmerized by his talks around the campfire. One week the group of children that arrived was deaf. They were a delight to be around and taught us some sign language which Helen and Becky still remember and use.

We spent about six weeks at the Circle Six that summer. The freshly painted signs were installed in their proper places, identifying different buildings for the campers. The Fourth Person rode out daily with the dude string in a circle around the ranch perimeter. Helen and Becky enjoyed the company of all the various children. The horses rested and ate well. We sold a couple more puppies to visitors, and that made for fewer mouths to feed as we headed west. Time was approaching for us to be on our way. We needed to be through the Rockies and across the continental divide before winter, and we were still in Texas.

A friend of Jerry Bob named Tommy Miracle of the nearby town of Snyder, had befriended us during our stay. He brought and loaned to us a small rubber wheeled wagon for us to tow behind the main wagon. It was set up for a team to pull, was much lighter, similar to a light freight wagon, but smaller. The inside of the wagon box had room for our water tank. We could now access water sources more easily. And make short runs without having to use the big wagon. Tommy lived up to his name. It was a miracle, and much needed. Mr. Miracle had a well drilling business in the town of Snyder. His motto was "If we find water it's a Miracle well!" Tommy was a typical tall lanky Texan with a big smile, and a heart the size of Texas.

A few days before we started west again, the dude string escaped from the corral and was found wandering close by, nibbling the grasses that grew around the bunkhouses. A shake of a bucket with a scoop of grain would have been all that was necessary to head them back into their confines. But the Fourth Person saddled up Rocky, and started whooping and hollering and chasing the horses at full speed around the church campgrounds. The children were still at breakfast when this commotion began, safely inside a building. Rocky was working up a pretty good sweat in the warm morning sun, trying to keep the now excited horses from turning back and having another fun frolic across the open fields between the bunkhouses. Finally the herd turned in submission and headed back to the gate they had escaped from. The Fourth Person riding Rocky galloped him behind the herd, then turned him to jump over a weed covered pile of dirt and large rocks for a cowboy style finish. Unseen in the pile of brush was a large concrete building block. As Rocky came down from the leap over the pile, his near hind foot landed inside of one of the two holes of the block. The sharp edge of the concrete cut deep into his leg above the fetlock. I arrived at the scene in time to see Rocky jump the pile and come down hard.

The extra wrangler working for the camp secured the escaped horses back in the pasture where they quickly went back to eating their hay. Rocky stood, kicking his injured leg as if to shake loose whatever it was that was stinging him. Blood was running freely and filling his hoof print as he walked. I grabbed a garden hose and ran the cool water down his leg. The cut was about four inches above the fetlock. I could see the tendon move up and down as he moved his leg. Rocky was sliced several inches around the back of his leg. This was bad. Really bad. I applied the same Furazone ointment we had for Dusty's fistula. The bleeding slowed, then stopped.

Two days later, the wound had swelled and Tommy Miracle graciously brought his trailer to take Rocky to the vet in Odessa. The doctor put Rocky in the stocks, gave him a sedative, and then carefully examined the wound. He said that the sheath enveloping the large tendon at the back of Rocky's leg was infected, and Rocky would need six months to recover. Now we had two horses with injuries. Dusty's fistula had not gotten any better. In fact it seemed worse. The money I had saved from the sign painting had barely covered Rock's vet bill. Broke again and two horses hurt. I felt helpless.

The next day, Tommy the miracle man showed up at the Circle Six with a cute strawberry roan Appaloosa mare named Buttons. He suggested we trade. He would take care of Rocky, and we could use Buttons. It would be good experience for the four-year-old mare to go on a trip like this. When Rocky was better, we'd meet up and switch. Rocky limped into Tommy Miracle's trailer. I didn't know that it would be over a year before I would see him again.

Before we left on the next leg of our journey, Tommy also brought us a team of matched blonde Belgian geldings. Their names were Tom and Jerry. They were bigger than Dusty and Dolly and a lot younger. Maybe four or five years old. Palomino colored with white manes and tails. They were still green broke, and the Fourth Person told Tommy he would finish their training, and have them pull the wagon for a few hundred miles to give them over the road experience. The only time either of them was harnessed was at the Circle Six. Fourth Person teamed the larger one of the two up with Dolly, and hooked them to an iron wheeled flat wagon used for hayrides. The racket of the iron wheels grinding on the single lane paved road around the campground upset the younger, larger horse. He sped up and tried to run, but Dolly, slow and steady kept him secured. The lines to the team were the same ones I used on Dusty and Dolly. And in much the same condition as the rest of our harness. They were old and weak. I was riding on the back of this wagon, along with Jerry Bob's teenage daughter. Fourth Person was sawing tightly back and forth on the lines in an effort to slow the panicky colt that was bouncing back and forth in his harness. I yelled forward that I didn't think it was a good idea to use so much force because the lines were old and weak. And as luck would have it, at the end of my sentence, a line to the blond gelding snapped and we had a runaway. I ordered my companion at the back of the wagon to jump off. I knew we were in for a run before it started, and it was safer to jump now than later. She hit the ground on her feet but twisted an ankle. I bailed off the side. The only connection now between the driver and the horses was to our old mare Dolly. She was not inclined to trot, let alone run, but the sheer strength of the larger horse at her side was no match. He literally drug her at a gallop back to the barn. That was the only time Tom or Jerry wore a harness. Though the time came when we needed a fresh team, Tom and Jerry just walked along side the wagon from Stanton to Lincoln, New Mexico. The Fourth Person was always going to start them tomorrow, and it never came.

With Rocky in the very capable hands of Tommy Miracle, a fresh team of young horses we could use (but didn't), Buttons the Appaloosa mare, and a small wagon for our water tank, we prepared to leave. Tommy also gave us a pair of collar pads for the mares, and a nice set of driving lines to use. The motorcycle we had towed at the back of the wagon was put in its place. There was still a cage full of pups under the wagon though fewer in number. We had more horses now than when we started. And less money. Roll call included Dusty and Dolly, Prince the Paint stallion, Burrito the Black, Taco, the blonde giants Tom and Jerry, Buttons the Appaloosa mare, the sorrel filly and the spotted pony. Ten head to care for, and we were heading into desert country.

The morning of our departure Burrito the Black was reluctant to be lead to his position at the back and rear of the wagon. He hadn't been handled at all during our stay and had been left to the freedom of the large dude string pasture, only coming in twice a day for food and water. He liked it there and would have been happy to stay. To force the issue, Fourth Person put a lariat rope loop around Burritos neck, and attempted to lead the strong black mule with a dally around the saddle horn while mounted on the spotted stallion, Prince. The stallion was a larger equine than the mule, but the mule was more powerful. As Burrito was drug close to the rear of the wagon, he jumped sideways and managed to get the motorcycle between him and the stallion. Everything that happened after that was a slow motion train wreck. The pile of wreckage included a motorcycle, a paint horse and a wild eyed mule in a huge tangled mess of rope, with the Fourth Person somewhere near the bottom. A true Kodak moment. But alas, I had no camera handy. After the dust settled and everyone gained their footing, Burrito took his place at the rear of the wagon. Amazingly again, there were no injuries. I suppose where there's no sense, there's no feeling.

A decision was made to leave the motorcycle behind in storage at the Circle Six. Thus far it had not been used and was just extra weight for the mares to pull. We then continued to prepare for our departure. I stepped up into the wagon to begin securing our personal belongings and as I did so I noticed several pots and black cast iron skillets that I didn't recognize. The building our wagon was parked next to was a bunkhouse with a kitchen. For some reason, the Fourth Person decided to help himself to some kitchenware. We certainly didn't need or even have room for the extra items. On top of that, they didn't belong to us. They belonged to the church camp. When I questioned the Fourth Person about it he admitted taking the items. As soon as he was busy elsewhere I put them back in the bunkhouse. This was an ongoing problem the Fourth Person had. He stole things. It really disgusted me and was very embarrassing, mostly because I was related to this person by marriage. I checked through the wagon for more contraband and satisfied that all was decent and in order, continued to prep the horses for the trip. It was not until we were a few days down the road that I discovered the quiver of arrows taken from Jerry Bob's storage room, and four Bibles, hidden above our bed in the top storage area. I had to question myself about the type of person that felt a need to steal Bibles from a church camp. It wasn't like he was going to *read* one. I felt really bad. Jerry Bob Taylor had been a gracious host for the last six weeks. We had been fed, and our horses fed. Bath and laundry facilities were at our disposal. We swam in the pool, and they transported us to town when needed. I had money for Rocky's injury because of Jerry Bob. In return, one of the members of our family deliberately stole from him. It was beyond my comprehension. It wasn't the first time this type of thing had happened. It wouldn't be the last.

After passing below the overhead gate of the Circle Six Ranch, I pointed the mares north. The same direction that horrific dust storm had come from. This part of Texas was farmland or wasteland, dotted with oil wells here and there. The population was spread out, and I had the feeling of open country ahead void of people. This area is called the Llano. Flat. Desolate. A country filled with rattlesnakes and tumbleweeds. We had left the humidity of the Hill Country long ago. It was dry and hot. The trees were few and far between and stunted for lack of rain. Water was going to be even more difficult to find. The towns that refreshed us were spread thin. At Lenorah we turned west. The asphalt road was just a two-lane farm road with a wide graded area on either side that I could pull over on, to let the occasional cars and trucks go by.

As we quietly continued down this road a farmer in a truck pulled up next to me and leaned out the passenger window. "You're dragging a mule back there". I told him "thank you." Fourth Person was riding Prince out ahead of the wagon about fifty feet off to the side of the wide shoulder. When he stopped and turned, he saw what the farmer had seen and ordered me to stop. I thought Burrito the Black was merely leaning back on his rope. It was the outrider's job to keep on eye on the animals that I couldn't see. The farmer was correct. We were dragging a mule. The black one. Flat out. Along the ground.

It's important when tying a horse, or in this case, a mule, to use the proper equipment. A halter is a humane horse head collar that the horse responds to when he's being led. It fits on the head in such a way that it does not tighten. Burrito the Blacks problem was not the halter. He was tied to the wagon with the lariat, left over from this morning's wreck. The lariat rope loop around his neck had tightened and cut off his air. He had a halter on, but it was not being used. The rope was looped around his neck, with the other end tied to the wagon. Burrito had passed out from lack of air and fell over, which did not cause the rope to loosen, but tighten still. It was hard to tell how long he had been dragging. The loop around his neck had tightened to less than a six-inch diameter. He was almost decapitated. No blood, but unbelievably constricted. Fourth Person galloped Prince up to the black carcass on the ground. I arrived by foot at the same time.

For a moment we both scanned the motionless mule. Burrito's one exposed eye stared motionless into the sky. I reached down and tried to loosen the rope but was not strong enough. I couldn't even get my fingers beneath it. The rope had buried itself deep into Burrito's neck. Fourth Person to the rescue. He yanked the rope viciously and loosened the strangle hold. Burrito gasped! His legs kicked in spasm. When the loop was loosened the rest of the way, Burrito lifted his head, then rolled up onto his legs. A few seconds later he jumped back to his feet and shook his head. His short black tail swished back and forth. It was resurrection day. It's not easy to kill a mule, even though we apparently had tried. I found a cotton lead rope and I snapped it onto Burritos halter so this would not happen again. Our first day out from our layover, and almost lost a mule. Not a good start. I wondered at the next thousand miles had in store for us and prayed for no loss of life.

Not far out of Lenorah, we stopped for the night. The horses were staked out along the highway eating the dried grasses available to them. The mules were always placed where the grass was the thinnest. Dolly and Dusty were put in an area with the most grass. Even with the lower feed available the mules were never thin. That evening a couple from the next burg of Tarzan stopped by and bought the spotted pony for their children. Helen had ridden the little guy many miles alongside the road and the pony was now broke and very gentle. We would buy Helen another pony to ride and train somewhere along the road ahead. I kept back enough money from the sale of this one to make sure we could get another. The rest we used for groceries, and a couple of bags of grain for the horses.

NEW MEXICO

Andrews, Texas was the last Texas town we would see. We stopped for groceries and ice. Hopefully enough to last us the two or three days it would take for us to make Eunice, almost forty miles ahead. The day we walked into New Mexico was just like any other. It took me back a bit to comprehend that we had walked halfway across Texas. I had plenty of time to ponder this as we steadily walked along the side of the road. The scenery remained the same. Flat, dry, with a steady breeze that barely bent the wild grasses in the open spaces to our left and right. From my high seat on the wagon, I could see over the top of Dusty and Dolly onto the pavement ahead. A flat white rope-like object lay in our path several yards ahead. The mares paid it no mind and walked directly over it. As it came nearer, I could see it was a snake or what was left of one. A big one, about six feet long. It had been run over so many times, that it was embedded into the asphalt. All that was left of it was the serpentine spine, flattened like a fossil and perfectly preserved into the blacktop of west Texas Hwy176.

There was a pleasant aroma of high desert now in the mornings. The wind that brought it blew gently, cooling the sweat that dripped off the mares' flanks. The scent of the horses sweat mingled with the oily harness and desert flowers as it drifted past me. Had I been able to bottle it, I would have named it Cowgirl Delight. It was indeed.

We were in New Mexico's southeastern corner. The sparse grass was dry and thin, but at night the horses were still eager to eat it. Water continued to be the constant target of my daily hunt. By studying a map I could see we would have a long stretch between Eunice and Carlsbad. There would be no town for a long seventy-mile stretch. No town meant no 'for sure' water. The map showed a narrow black line going across nearly featureless white paper. It would be a desolate walk. I was very concerned about water.

It was June, and hot. I had wanted to be up in the mountains by now, but the stop at the Circle Six had put us back. Not that we had a schedule per se, but reaching Prescott before winter was a must. The Rocky Mountains were no place to be if a hard winter snowstorm hit. Visions of the Donner party danced in my head.

Dolly and Dusty plodded along. We had a rhythm again. The horses knew it well. Eat at night. Walk all day. Drink whenever it was offered. Walk down the endless highway. I enjoyed the gentle sway of the wagon. Its rubber wheels cushioned the shock of the road. In the afternoon the girls would sometimes take a nap, read or color in their coloring books while we progressed down the side of the blacktop at a steady four miles per hour. I sometimes pondered if another family, back in the 1800's had come down this trail and how much more difficult and dangerous it would have been for them. We were not concerned about wild Indians or outlaws. The closest outlaw was in fact, riding the paint stallion alongside the wagon. There were Indians ahead but they were friendly. Feed and water were the issue. But mostly water. We were slowly approaching a three-day walk with only enough water for a day. The furthest distance we had covered in a day thus far was twenty-two miles. Normally we would travel no more than fifteen.

That meant we had to average over twenty-three miles a day...or else. I'm certain if needed I could have flagged down a local rancher and had some water delivered. As of yet we had not gotten ourselves into such a desperate situation, and I preferred to keep it that way.

We had an extra passenger along for the ride since we left the Circle Six. His name was Dusty, just like the mare on the left. His parents had brought him from their home in Big Spring and dropped him off the morning we left the church camp. Dusty slept on the floor in the front of the wagon. He learned how to drive the team, and we let him ride the gentle stallion alongside the wagon. This was an adventure of a lifetime for a young man of fourteen. Dusty helped harness the team, water and care for the horses. And he never complained. Even when he had to bathe in a cold cattle water tank. He had the heart of a pioneer. At the end of his two-week expedition tears streaked his sun kissed cheeks as he waved goodbye. Oh, how I would have preferred to have kept Dusty and sent Fourth Person back with his parents instead.

The horse Dusty was still plagued by the infection on her neck. It was doctored routinely. The collar pad from Tommy Miracle kept the leather from rubbing the wound. There was no longer *any* weight from the wagon tongue pressing down. The tongue had been tied up at the proper height to the wagon with a motorcycle strap. Neither horse would bear its weight. Still, the wound never closed and seeped continually.

The morning we left Eunice, we topped off the water tank and filled every bucket we could find with water. The buckets had no lids. Some of the water sloshed out when we hit a bump on the road. Still we would need every drop we could carry. That evening came with only eighteen miles traveled. Five short of the daily average we should have done. It was a dry camp. We watered the horses from the buckets and then drew water from the tank. The mules got a half ration. Then we staked them all out alongside the lonely highway for the evening. It had been hot that day, but I would be satisfied with an evening bath of just a wet wash cloth. The girls washed their hands in the rubber tub and I wiped their sweaty faces. We ate a simple one-skillet dinner of boiled noodles mixed with a can of mushroom soup, peas and tuna.

The next morning we were back on the road earlier than usual. Dusty the boy was a great help when it came to the routine of watering and prepping the horses. There were a lot of mouths to water. Each horse would be led to a bucket to drink their fill in the morning. Then tied to their place on the wagon. Prince and Buttons were saddled. Even if they wouldn't be ridden just to lighten the wagonload, if only by a few pounds. Taco wore a small packsaddle and carried a light load in two small bags. The yearling sorrel filly, Burrito the Black, and Tom and Jerry were neither saddled nor harnessed. The water wagon behind was much lighter now that most of the water was gone. It was day two of our three-day stretch across the New Mexico desert. If we didn't find water tonight, the horses would go thirsty.

My seat on the wagon was shielded from the sun in the morning. We were heading west and the morning sun was directly behind us. Heat waves began to roil in the distance. A mirage of water appeared on the horizon across the road we followed. The terrain occasionally had small rolling hills though the road remained flat. We were highly visible from a long way off. A bright red box against a sea of cream colored sand and dirt following an endless gray strip of pavement. The sparse traffic on the highway gave us a wide berth and seldom slowed. Ranch land flanked us, stretching off to the north and south horizons with no sign of human habitation. A fence of endless barbed wire stretched east and west as far as you could see. This was desolation at its finest. Even the melodies of birds had stopped. The big mares' rubber shoes made hollow clopping sounds as they walked. The smaller horses shod with iron produced a higher pitched ringing as they clapped upon the pavement. The harness trace chains jingled. The wagons creaked and groaned. The horses' tails swished as if conducting this traveling orchestra. The same song played for us all day long. And yet, I never grew tired of it.

The mileage signs posted along the roadside kept track of our progress. At midday the horses got a swallow of water out of a bucket that was brought to them. They all wanted more, but there was none to be had. Just as we passed the marker notifying me of the twentieth mile we had walked that day, I spotted a windmill. It was off the highway to the south on the ranch side of the highway fence. As we got closer I could see a faint dirt two track leading off the highway to it. A barbed wire gate in the highway fence was the only access. The Fourth Person opened it and rode through to check out the water available. There was no fresh water, just a dirt cow tank with the leftover of a past rain in the bottom. The windmill had not been used in quite awhile. Dirty water was better than none, and the horses weren't picky. Each one was untied and led down to the cow tank to drink their fill. In the morning they all got to drink again. There would be no water for anyone until we made Carlsbad, thirty-two miles away.

The next day I searched continually in all directions, hoping we would find water along the road, but that was not the case. Each mile we passed was dry and desolate. Ten miles, no water, fifteen miles, no water. At noon we stopped for just a few minutes. The horses expected a sip, but got nothing. Even our seventeen-gallon Gerry can was dry. At twenty miles the horses started showing fatigue. They dropped their heads lower, resigned to their fate. One foot in front of the other. Still we walked on. The sun was blazing hot that day in late June. No longer sheltered from the sun, I slowly roasted in the afternoon sun. I could feel my face getting sunburned. Sunscreen was a luxury item we did not have. I didn't even own a hat. I had Helen soak a washcloth in the melted ice at the bottom of the Styrofoam ice chest and bring it to me. After wiping my face I left the damp cloth lay around my neck. The mares were slowing from their usual pace. We had to keep going. In the distance I could see signs of civilization. We were still ten miles out. The afternoon was turning to evening. It would take more than two hours for us to cover the distance. The sun was not far from the horizon when we passed the 'Welcome to Carlsbad' sign. It would be dark soon, and we needed a place to camp, rest, and let the horses recover. I prayed we would not have to drive through town to the other side to find a campsite. It would be dark before we could make it. Our horses were spent. We had traveled thirty-two miles that day.

To my left in the distance I could see evidence of water. Perhaps a creek or stream. We turned left at the next road and found a spot with tall green grass and a narrow stream of running water. A flat spot large enough to stop the wagon appeared. Dusty and Dolly walked slowly into it and stopped. Their sides were streaked with lines of salty white sweat. I worked quickly to get them unhooked and led to the little stream. The big nostrils flared as their lips dropped into the cool wetness, and they sucked in long delicious gulps. Then pulling them away after a few sips I let them eat some of the tall grass. A few minutes later, I allowed them to drink again. This time when their heads came up, they were ready to eat. With an old coffee can I splashed a little water on their backs, then tied them out for the night. The other horses were led to water and scattered out for the evening across the lowland by the stream. It was well after dark before I made dinner that night, cooking by Coleman light on the Coleman stove. The next morning we let the horses drink and changed them to fresh spots for grazing. Again I cleaned and doctored Dust's chronic wound. A newspaper reporter showed up that day wrote an article about us. I had mentioned that under different circumstances I would have liked to take the girls to the Carlsbad Caverns. It was not feasible with our mode of transportation. I never saw the article in the paper, but the reporter must have mentioned it. Before we broke camp later that week, a couple found us and made arrangements for us to go to the Caverns. They drove us there, paid for admission for all, and took us back to the wagon and horses at the end of our visit. The Caverns were a delightful respite from the heat. We walked down and down into its damp coolness. Helen and Becky marveled at the rock formations. I delighted in the underground pools of cold, clear water. We spent the entire day underground, awed by the unlimited formations of limestone hidden deep in the earth. This was a wonderful field trip away from our own adventure. At the end of the underground trail was a much-welcomed elevator to the top.

Figure 5. Dolly with the girls in Carlsbad, New Mexico.

The next town of any size was the borough of Artesia. What a refreshing sounding name for a town. Artesia. Just the word promised an abundance of water. Artesia was a mere 36 miles away. Half the distance we had traversed between Eunice and Carlsbad. It seemed like a cakewalk compared to that. And water should be readily available. The horses had rested several days to recover their strength. Then we harnessed up and headed north.

A few miles out of town, a truck pulling a two-horse trailer pulled to the side of the road and waited for our slow approach. It was a police officer that had visited us at our campsite in Carlsbad. He asked us on his earlier visit if we could let his young mare walk along with us for the day. Of course, we were happy to fill his request. Young horses need new experiences to round out their education. In one single day, a horse traveling with us would learn about leading, being part of a herd, equine etiquette, traffic, highway signs, harnesses, loud noises, barking dogs, wagons, stop lights, people, things that flap in the wind, and how to eat and drink when it was offered. Like children, horses behave better when they're a little bit tired. Feed them, let them nap. Keep their minds working. Today, most children *and* horses have too little work and too much free time on their hands, or hooves, whichever the case may be. This leads to bad behavior. With a rebellious child, you can fold them over to straighten them out. Horses don't fold very well. They must be trained.

In order to train one, it's easier if you speak their language. They *do* have a language. Not verbal, but body language. Horses understand each other. When you understand their language, you will understand the horse. Putting a young horse in with seasoned horses allows the younger one to learn from the older ones. This is what we did with the dropped off mare. She spent the day walking alongside the wagon, with Prince walking in front of her, and Burrito the Black trailing behind. The fourteen miles or so she walked was the longest outing she had ever been on. When the other horses started walking, she did too. When they stopped, she did too. And all the time she was surrounded with ever changing scenery and commotion. None of the horses or mules around her snorted, bucked or danced sideways. Everyone just walked calmly down the road, and so did she. Her wild eyes and snorts disappeared after the first mile. She became part of the herd. That evening when her ride pulled up at our campsite, she happily jumped into the trailer and buried her nose in the hay that awaited her. I'm sure she slept well that night.

The next afternoon we arrived on the outskirts of Artesia, New Mexico. The two-lane road we traveled on was bladed widely on both sides of the pavement. When the shoulders of a road were wide and flat, and graded as this was, I drove the wagon onto it and off the pavement. It made for a bumpier ride, but got our slow moving obstruction off the highway completely. A small concrete irrigation canal followed alongside the road on the right. It was running nearly to the top with crystal clear fresh water. I pulled the horses closer to this man-made stream and stopped the wagon. It was a pause that refreshed. Buckets were dipped in the rushing water and all the animals drank until they wanted no more. The water tank in the small wagon we pulled behind was topped off. In the midst of our stop, a car pulled in and a young man greeted me. He told me he was a photographer and asked permission to photograph the horses. I assured him that was certainly fine with us and he then set about taking pictures. He thanked us when he was finished, and promised to catch us on the road somewhere with copies. I didn't think much more about it, but he was good to his word. It is his photo of Dusty that appears on the front of this book. He caught her in the midst of a big yawn. It's a miracle that this photo even exists. In 1989, just two months after I dropped the Fourth Person back at his parent's house to live without me, all the photos were destroyed when the trailer I was living in burned to the ground. The few photos shown in this book were taken by or in the possession of friends or family. We passed through Artesia and camped a few miles out of town. The next morning a farmer from across the road stopped and accused us of stealing a bale of hay from his barn a half mile away. Yes, it was true that there was a thief among us. However our horses had no hay to eat, or was a bale present, nor the evidence of one recently consumed. The horses were still on their tie out ropes busily eating the native grasses that grew alongside the road. After a few harsh words, the farmer left. I resented the accusation. Had he known the nature of the Fourth Person he would have turned his investigation elsewhere. The only way a bale of hay could have been absconded by our own traveling crook was by physically dragging it the entire distance of the half-mile. This was improbable, as Fourth Person found it beyond his capacities to pick up aluminum cans along the road. On top of that, he had no interest in providing the horses with their daily dietary intake. That was my responsibility.

That next evening camp was just beyond the town of Lake Arthur. As we unharnessed and were tying the horses out for the evening a couple drove up, stopped, and asked us if we would be interested in buying a pony. They gave us a ride back to their home and introduced us to Peter Pony. The smoky gray Shetland only pulled his head up for a moment to acknowledge our presence. His focus was on the overgrown zucchini squash at his feet. He had let himself into their backyard garden area and was gourmet dining. No reservations either. Not with Peter Pony! He helped himself to the horn of plenty spread around him like a Baptist at a church potluck. Peter focused again on the zucchini, opening his jaws as wide as possible to surround the green monster with his mouth and like a shark, left a terrible gaping hole in the vegetables flesh. Peter Pony raised his head with his victim still in his teeth. Both ends fell back to the ground and foam fell from the pony's mouth as he devoured his prey. The little predator could be ours for three, twenty-dollar bills. His owners told us Peter was eight years old, and may or may not be broke. And that he 'might buck' when you rode him. Their children had been led around on his back a few times. I never checked his teeth to have an idea of his age. It wasn't important as we would probably sell him when the opportunity arose, and buy yet another. He looked to be in his prime. Fat and Shetland sassy. Helen had a new pony to ride.

Normally when we sold a horse, we used the money to buy supplies and food. If possible, we saved part of the money to purchase another horse, or in this case a pony, with the intention of reselling him when the opportunity arose. Buy low. Sell high. Use the profit to live on and buy another in order to repeat the process. It was one of the ways we made money, though it didn't happen very often. Peter Pony became a member of our traveling band the next day and stayed with us until he died at a very old age nearly twenty years later.

The first day we let Peter walk along with the group to get the hang of things. He was a smart little feller. He stood about forty inches tall, was charcoal gray with a light mane and tail. His color is technically called silver dapple. Peter Pony was saddled the next morning and when Helen climbed aboard Peter he proceeded to buck and behave badly. Helen jumped off before she was thrown. The Fourth Person reached Peter about the time Helen landed. He reached over Peter's back and grabbed the pony by his flank, just as the calf ropers do, lifted Peter off his feet and threw him on his side to the ground. The sandy soil cushioned the fall. I feared he would have broken a rib otherwise. Fourth Person held the pony down and pounded on him with his fist. Helen cried. Becky ran back into the wagon, and I hollered 'Stop it!' Fourth Person checked his anger and Peter Pony was allowed back to his feet. Crying, Helen walked back over and resumed her place in the saddle. She directed Peter away from the wagon, and the Fourth Person's angry gaze. Both were happy to escape the menace standing there. I don't know if Peter connected Helen with being his savior, but the two bonded that day, and Peter never bucked again. She rode him all that day. Trotting alongside the wagon, sometimes galloping out ahead. The opportunity to sell Peter never arose, and I was glad of it. Helen had her very own pony. She rode him nearly everyday.

Peter had feet like iron and never needed shod. He walked the whole distance barefoot. The mules also went barefoot. Taco had tough little feet like Peter Pony. So did Burrito the Black. They managed to trim themselves as they walked. That was a good thing, as I don't think Fourth Person would have had much luck hammering a shoe onto the half-wild mule. The other saddle horses were shod with regular iron shoes as needed. When a shoe fell off along the trail, we allowed the horse to walk without it for a few days. The result was a perfectly trimmed hoof, nearly ready for the new shoe. I must give credit where credit is due. Fourth Person did all the shoeing. He only allowed one horse on the trip to go barefoot so long her feet started to bleed. A yearling Shetland filly. We picked her up and put her on the wagon at that point and she rode first class on the front porch until she recovered.

The draft horses were a different matter. Dusty and Dolly wore number five size draft horse shoes. They were scarce as hen's teeth. The hard asphalt and mileage wore them out quickly, and replacements were difficult to find. Instead, Fourth Person found old rubber car tires and cut their shoes out of the tread. This was rather ingenious. I wish I could say it was his own idea, but another traveler had passed it along to him. The tires were thick and cushioned the big mare's feet while giving them great traction on the pavement. These shoes were not cut into a u shape as an actual horseshoe, but left as a solid pad covering the entire bottom of the hoof. A square shaped piece of tread was cut from the flat bottom of a rubber tire and nailed to the hoof, then the excess trimmed off like grandma paring the crust off her homemade pie. The biggest problem was that these pads worked themselves off the nails within a week or two, and continually had to be reset. The tires themselves rarely wore out and could be used over and over again. Goodyears, Michelins, and Uniroyals. That's how we rolled.

Two days after Peter Pony joined us we walked into Roswell and turned west on Hwy 380 towards Capitan, Lincoln, and Ruidoso. As evening approached I started scouting for a suitable campsite. The right side of the highway was too narrow to pull the wagon safely off to the side. Just off the shoulder, the right of way between the pavement and the highway perimeter fence sloped steeply upwards. The wider left side was slightly downhill and showed the effects of receiving the preponderance of the highway rainwater runoff. Not only was the grass greener on the other side, but there was plenty of space to park the wagon away from the pavement. The trick would be to get the wagon off the steeper edge of the shoulder into the flat area below. If met at an angle, the top heavy wagon box could tip over. I would have to hit the far shoulder straight on, at a right angle to the pavement. The slope down was only a drop of two or three feet, but if hit at an angle, it could be a major problem.

I waited until traffic from both directions was far off, and swung Dusty and Dolly to the left, across the oncoming traffic lane and hit the gravel on the far side at a perfect angle. The mares stepped down into the grass just off the shoulder and the wagon jerked to a sudden stop. We were high centered on a piece of steel jutting out below the wagon tongue where it attached to the wagon. It had dug itself deep into the hard gravel. I clucked at Dusty and Dolly again and they jerked against their trace chains. We were stuck fast. The big red wagon sat sideways in the east bound slow lane. The smaller wagon with the water tank with the blonde draft geldings Tom and Jerry tied behind it blocked traffic beyond the centerline. Together we made a long and colorful roadblock that could have slowed any fleeing convicts being chased by the law. We had sufficiently closed down three lanes of a four-lane highway. The visions that raced through my head made no room for any further catastrophes. I told Helen and Becky to get out of the wagon and stand by the far off highway fence. Now! They obediently complied and stood watching as cars slowed and began backing up along the road. I didn't know how things could get any worse. Fourth Person was angrily yelling at me as he tried to dig the buried steel out of the gravel with his hands. "Try again" he yelled and I encouraged Dusty and Dolly to get serious this time. They bounced into their collars like a team at a draft horse pull. Back and forth they jumped, and then the weakest part gave way. Dolly's wooden single tree broke right in two. It snapped like a dry rotted twig. I calmed the mares. Now we really had a problem.

I dropped the lines and ran to the small wagon tied behind. At least we could roll that one out of the way. We unhooked it and rolled it down onto the grass complete with Tom and Jerry, and Taco and Peter. Some of the backed up traffic could get around us now. Fourth Person changed out the single tree from the small wagon to the large while I moved the other saddle horses tied to the main wagon to the grassy bottom and secured them. When I climbed back up on the wagon seat, the steel rod had been sufficiently dug out so that the mares could break it through the last few inches. We quietly rolled down into the flat grassy area as if nothing ever happened. I stopped the mares and they dropped their heads into the deep grass to graze. Then I jumped off the wagon and shakily walked to the barbed wire fence separating the highway from the ranch land beyond, fell to my knees and vomited. It had been a stressful twenty minutes.

Caring for the horses that evening helped ease my anxiety. All had plenty of tall green grass to munch on throughout the night. The large water tank was full and all had plenty of water. Dinner was burritos again, but no one seemed to mind. Just before dark a small white truck pulled up and a young couple got out to visit. Their names were Karen and Lee. Apparently they had been following our progress for awhile and wanted to meet the strange wagon travelers. When darkness overtook us, we all climbed up onto the flat top of the wagon via the built in ladder on the front porch. There we sat under the stars and listened to Karen play her guitar and sing 'Dust in the Wind'. We had no radio or television and we all found this live entertainment refreshing.

Helen and Becky lay on the wagon's roof and eagerly watched for falling stars and UFOs. The sky was black and the twinkling white frost of the Milky Way stretched across it from horizon to horizon. Occasionally a car from the highway with its obnoxious lights would interrupt our gazing at the universe in complete darkness. The sound of its engine broke the quiet stillness of the night until it faded again into the distance. Then the only sounds were of the horses and mules breathing, nibbling their grass, and the occasional clink of a lead snap on a halter ring. We stared up into the universe trying to comprehend its immensity. A verse from the book of Psalms crossed my thoughts. "He stretched out the heavens...." Yes, He certainly did.

The next morning we easily made our way back onto the highway without mishap, and once again faced west. In the distance I could see the foothills of the western Rockies along the horizon. The road had a slight but steady incline. The horses pulling the wagon were working a little harder.

The old mare Dolly troubled me. She had a condition commonly referred to as 'roaring', or 'windbroke'. The farmer that sold the team to us failed to tell us about it. At sometime in Dolly's past, someone had overworked and overheated her to the point of scarring her larynx. When really put to a strenuous workout, such as a long steep hill, the scarring in her windpipe would not allow it to expand so that she could take in enough air for her exertion. The result would be a roaring sound. Wheezing... like an asthmatic.

An animal that weighed nearly seventeen hundred pounds gasping for air resonated louder than a colony of Darth Vader impersonators. There was no question as to when she was close to her limit. So when I heard the deep rattling sounds begin, I always pulled the wagon to the side of the road and stopped until all was back to normal. Dolly usually recovered in less than five minutes and we could proceed. Had she not been allowed to catch her breath things would escalate to a crisis situation, at which time Dolly would pass out from lack of oxygen. The thought of another Burrito the Black incident was enough to keep my attention on the welfare of the old mare. Because we lived with the horses all day every day, I was attuned to their needs. Any tiny thing out of the ordinary with any of them would set off my radar and I would take care of whatever it was as soon as possible. But mostly, on the day to day basis it was just the endless search for food and water. Nothing brought me greater comfort than to know they had plenty of grass to eat and water available. There were a lot of mouths to feed.

The road kept winding upwards. We were along side of a four-lane highway creeping towards the next place on the map known as Riverside. As the highway entered into the foothills, it swung in a crescent moon shape to the pass high above us. The climb looked to be more than a mile long, and it was steeper that anything we had traveled. A guardrail on the right side of the road had no openings for pullouts along its climb. We would be walking on the paved shoulder until we reached the summit. If we had to stop, for whatever reason, we would still be on the pavement. Just before the climb commenced, I pulled the wagon off the road and let everyone rest for what lay ahead. It was midday and the weather was warm, but not yet hot. A bucket of water was passed around for the horses to sip from. Then we slowly rolled back out onto the road and the team immediately went to work. Fourth Person had tied onto the tongue with the Appaloosa mare Buttons. We had three horses pulling, but this would have been a tough job for four. And I knew Dolly would give out before we reached the top. Half way up Dolly started to rattle. I pulled her back and pushed Dusty further into her collar to make up for the loss of her helper. Dusty was determined to dig in and do the job. Buttons was keeping the rope tight and pulling her share of the load. The old mare was not getting her wind back, as just the act of walking uphill without a load was taxing her. She started to stagger back and forth as she walked. We had to stop. I halted the horses and put my leg against the brake. Dolly just stood, sides heaving, gasping for air.

We were in dangerous place stopping where we were. The four-lane highway was busy that day but there was nothing else we could do. Dusty was dripping from the hard pull and grateful for the break. Buttons also had sweat trickling off her sides and legs. The summit looked a long ways off. Oh, how I wished we had put one of the young blonde geldings into the harness this morning. I would not make Dolly go through this again. We would swap places with them at the summit. Ten minutes rest seemed like an eternity along the busy highway. Hundreds of cars and trucks passed by. Dolly had recovered somewhat and we really needed to get to a safer place, so I clucked at the team and we continued. Dolly began roaring again a few hundred feet up the road. I stopped the team again, but this time only for a few minutes. Then continued on. The steepness of the highway started to lessen as we approached the summit. Dolly was still in trouble, but the load had lessened and she walked with effort to the top. She was wobbling as she stepped off the pavement onto a large gravel pullout at the top of the hill. We made it. Barely.

As soon as the last horse was safely onto the dirt in the pullout, I stopped the wagon and turned around to scan the valley below us. It spread outward to the horizon onto the Great Plains. From the top you could see Roswell in the distance and grasp the elevation climbed to create such a view. The rolling grass covered plains stretched out to the north, south, and east in an Oz type panorama. The air carried the scent of dried grasses, and auto emissions, the sound of flying insects and straining engines as they reached the summit. It had been a long stressful climb for all. Dolly's sides heaved in and out like a bellows. She shook where she stood. Buttons was soaking wet with sweat as was Dusty. Droplets fell from their fetlocks onto the dry dirt below. The other horses were breathing through their flared nostrils from the work out, but not sweating. The mules were neither sweating nor breathing hard. Evidence of their hybrid vigor.

The girls got out to explore the edges of the parking area. It was large, perhaps a half-acre graded area at the top of the hill. While we rested there a car pulled in, and once again, relatives climbed out. This time it was Fourth Person's younger sister and her husband. They were on their way to visit the people we had left at the beginning and they had been hoping to find us along the way. She wanted to know if they could take Helen and Becky back for a short visit and return them on their way back though. And just like that, Helen and Becky were waving goodbye through the back window of the car as they pulled back out on the highway. It was the first time on this trip my daughters would not be with me and I felt their absence. They would be gone for almost a week. I missed them already.

With a feeling of melancholy I clucked to the team and pointed them back onto the highway. We would find a suitable site and camp as early tonight as possible. The horses needed rest. As we wound our way down into Riverside we were met by a young man who claimed to be Billy the Kid. And apparently he was. At least he was the actor who would be portraying the young outlaw at the upcoming Billy the Kid Days in Lincoln. Billy wanted us to be there for the event and when we told him that we wouldn't be able to travel the necessary fifteen miles by morning, he made arrangements to have our whole rig and horses picked up the next day. That next morning not one of the horses hesitated walking into the trailer. They were all ready to ride for awhile. They had earned a rest. It was the only time on the trip west we caught a ride for any distance. The wagon was hooked onto by a pick up and off we went, covering the next fifteen miles in style! They settled us into a large apple orchard, just across the street from the famous jail that Billy the Kid escaped from. Water was available from a spigot, much to my delight, and there was sufficient grass for the horses. It was a nice place to spend a few days.

We settled right in and enjoyed the festivities. Karen and Lee showed up that weekend with an abundant supply of cantaloupes from a farm Lee had worked at. They were sweet and refreshing. Fresh fruits and vegetables were not our normal fare. We made a few dollars giving wagon rides in the smaller wagon, and Peter pony supplied small children with pony rides. I sold some note cards and belt buckles.

Tommy Miracle showed up with a trailer to pick up his geldings. Fourth Person had not fulfilled his obligation with Tommy to work with the geldings and I felt bad. The young team certainly got plenty of road experience, but never the driving training that was promised by fourth person. Fourth Person told Tommy that he would do it, and like many other things just never got around to it. This was another of Fourth Persons character traits. No reason to do today what you can put of till tomorrow and tomorrow is still tomorrow the next day. Whatever the reason I always felt ashamed for his actions or lack thereof.

I had expected to see Rocky arrive with Tommy that day, but Tommy said he was not healed up well enough to make the trip, and had needed more veterinary care. We were to keep the mare Buttons until the next time, and continue using her as we saw fit. It was all good experience for the young mare. She was sure enough kid broke already, and we were happy to keep her.

By the end of the week Helen and Becky had been returned. It was good to have my girls back. They loved the large apple orchard and played in the shade of the trees. It was also a favorite place for deer to frequent. One evening I saw a group of does close by, apparently accustomed to the proximity of town. They were grazing away from us, just beyond the staked out horses. I decided to see how close I could get to one that had just walked behind a short hedge of blackberries. When she dropped her head, I took a step, crouched, waited for her head to drop again and cautiously took another step. Five minutes passed. I had closed the distance by half. This was fun! Another five minutes had me close to the hedge. The wind must have been blowing the right direction. I'm certainly no hunter. But there she was, less than ten feet away, on the other side of the hedge. I watched her through the foliage. I was delighted to be so close to this beautiful wild thing. Her large ears flicked back and forth to discourage the flies. I could see the moisture on her nose. She moved closer to the wall of blackberries; parallel to the place I crouched behind. My legs were tingling now, from squatting low, but I dared not move. I barely breathed. I cautiously wound my arm through the brambles like a serpent, quietly, silently. The doe's flank was less than three feet away. Her head was down. As my hand broke through the far side the tips of my middle three fingers brushed against the stiff hair of her thigh. She never knew I was there. I was part of the black-berries. The doe walked on. When she had gone several yards I finally stretched out my cramping legs and she bolted. She stopped about forty feet away and turned to identify the menace from a safer distance. When I stood up, she bounded away with the others that had been grazing in the area, now alerted to my proximity. What an experience!

Some years later I was able to sneak up behind a java-lina near our home in Coyote Springs. The wind was blowing briskly that day the right direction, and javalinas with such poor eyesight are not difficult to stalk. I got close enough to grab it by the hind leg, but instead took a picture of it with the camera I held. Wise. Very wise. Javalinas have very sharp teeth and it's never a good idea to pick one up. The experience would be similar to putting your arm in a chipper/shredder. I still have the photo, and all my fingers.

Figure 6. The Coyote Springs Javalina.

Lincoln is a quaint tiny town nestled in the central mountains of New Mexico. It reeks of colorful history. The scenery around the town is inspiring. I could have stayed there. But our goal was Arizona, so once again we harnessed up and prepared for the trip further west. The decision was made to add an extra team to pull the wagon through the mountains. Having Dolly was like having an engine that only hit on half the cylinders. We needed more horsepower. But the most logical horses, Tom and Jerry, were gone. Now we had to pick from what we had available. The stallion Prince was an obvious choice. He was already broke to drive. That gave us three. Burrito the Black was too small for the harness, as was Peter pony and Taco the mini mule. That left the yearling, once again, too small and young, and Buttons. So Buttons was drafted, literally. We had a team harness to fit a saddle horse size team. Prince was harnessed. Buttons had never worn a harness before, nor pulled a wagon. I walked up to her that morning and said "Buttons, this is a collar" and secured it on her neck. Next came the rattling harness, which she accepted without a second glance.

Two hundred miles on the trail will certainly gentle a horse down. Dusty and Dolly were hooked to the wagon, and Prince and Buttons were placed in the front as the lead team. Problem was, they weren't leaders. They were followers. As soon as I said "giddup," Dusty and Dolly moved forward, and Prince and Buttons went separate directions. Not in a panic, just confused. We untangled the mess and tried again. This just wasn't working. We swapped places with the Belgians and the smaller team. Now Dusty and Dolly were in the lead. We rolled. It was a beautiful thing. Buttons never knew she was pulling a wagon. She was just walking along with her friends. By the end of the day, she knew her cues and was an old pro. Technically speaking, the larger team, known as the wheelers, should be at the rear. We were going against the norm, but the important thing was that we were going, which is the result we needed. And as it turned out, Buttons was not the only horse I trained to drive that way. The place where Buttons walked, in front of the wagon, behind the large team, and separated from the highway traffic by her own teammate, was the perfect place to put a horse new to driving. They were surrounded. There was nowhere to go. Once their harness was secured to the doubletree behind, and the neck yoke in front, they were trapped in a walking treadmill. It didn't take long for them to learn to maintain the same speed as the horses in front of them and at the side. Twenty miles further down the road Buttons and Prince were acting like old pros.

The drive away from Lincoln was beautiful. I was glad Buttons was behaving herself so that I could admire the scenery surrounding us. What a pleasant change from the desert we had recently left. The short distance to the next town of Capitan took less than a day to cover. We stopped for groceries at a small market along our route, then made our camp several miles out of town. Capitan was one of those charming small towns I could have been at home in. I liked it even better than the town of Lincoln.

That evening's camp had a nice yard-wide mountain stream running alongside the road. It was accessible through the barbed wire fence that separated the highway from the range land. I slipped through it and carried buckets of water for all the stock, water for washing some clothes, and baths for almost everyone. The next morning the girls and I put the little scrub board in the large horse tub and washed all our clothing. Once again, the barbed wire fence improvised as a clothes line. The grass was plentiful here and the horses spent the morning grazing along their tether lines. Beyond the stream about three hundred yards away, was a tall outcropping of rock that seemed to have a small cave entrance in the midst of it. The girls went with Fourth Person to hunt for arrowheads there. Helen and Becky did not come back disappointed and showed me some obsidian chips they had discovered. Not quite arrowheads, but the suggestion of some in the process of being made. They were delighted with their treasures.

After a day of rest we once again harnessed both the teams and headed west. The road led us out of the mountains and back onto the high plains near Carrizozo. We camped that night just past a lone house along a deserted stretch of the road. The owner of which came out and introduced himself. He then offered us water for our horses from a fifty-gallon barrel in his backyard that collected water from his windmill. Another neighbor stopped by, and purchased an original drawing from me. It was a nice ten by twelve pencil drawing depicting a rodeo cowboy riding a saddle bronc. I invited him to stay for dinner that evening. The fine dining I presented him with was one we had eaten many times. Boiled wide egg noodles, mixed with a can of tuna, a can of cream of mushroom soup, and a can of peas. It was the best I could offer. He graciously cleaned his paper plate and invited us to stop by his home in the morning. It was just down the road a few miles on the right.

Before we finished hooking up the teams the next morning a couple came and bought the yearling sorrel filly. She had been with us from the beginning, and had never been any trouble. I was sad and happy to see her go. Any life would be better than one traveling with us. I hoped she would have a good home. Her new owners seemed to be very nice and had other horses. The filly was very well bred with Clabber Bars and Top Deck on her papers. She would grow into a beautiful mare. It was also nice to have a few extra dollars so that we could buy some hay wherever possible. The natural grasses were not as lush as they had been and as we trekked west might disappear completely.

We were met a few miles away by the gentleman that had dined with us the night before. He insisted we pull up in front of his house, so that he could show me where his new drawing would be displayed. It had been a long time since I had been in a real home. This one was recently built, had the usual carpet and air conditioning, and was very well kept. While inside I gazed at the nicely decorated room where my picture would hang. There was a matching sofa and love seat in the living room. Drapes on the windows. The large cheerful kitchen had a breakfast bar with stools. Had I been in a palace I would not have been any more perplexed. I pondered to myself how it was possible for people come up with the money to pay for such a place. It was beyond my comprehension. My worldview was one of poverty and subsistence living. Regular paychecks were not a part of my reality. For a fleeting moment I allowed myself to fantasize about raising my daughters in a home like this one, but quickly dismissed it from my mind. I instead chose to be grateful for the wagon parked out front. There were places to call home that were worse than a horse drawn wagon. I knew this from experience. I counted my blessings and pushed that thing called hope back into the basement of my heart, and buried it there in a box, beneath the floor, hidden.

We had not made it to the town of Carrizozo before another equine joined our entourage. A woman approached us that had a mini mule for sale. A few dollars later, we had our third mule. He was a cute little thing. The same size as Taco, but much stockier. He was a pretty copper color with a chocolate color stripe down his back. It only made sense to add to our menu, so we dubbed him Enchilada. We would not run out of food now, for we had a Burrito, a Taco and an Enchilada. He assumed the position left open by the sorrel filly we had just sold. Enchilada was tied to the small wagon at the rear of our caravan.

Carrizozo was a small town spread out along the crossroads of two lonely highways. Beyond it to the west was the Valley of Fire. The road through this place was surrounded by a large flow of black basalt lava. It extended a total of forty miles from tip to tip. As we walked slowly pass this cremated slice of earth, I contemplated the catastrophic event that took place here thousands of years ago. Chipmunks and lizards stared at us from the peaks of the black rock just beyond the barbed wire highway fence. The lava flows formed an unending variety of shapes, some taller than our wagon. Occasionally large globs of magma had pushed up, then splintered as it cooled and fractured into mazes. Others appeared as giant slices of black cheese pointing towards the sky. A few brave grasses and daring yucca found footholds between their cracks. Malapai boulders were strewn throughout. The most interesting were the giant layers of black ooze that appeared like a massive cake batter poured out on the prairie floor. In the midst of this natural calamity were birds, reptiles and rodents. Their fortress was impenetrable. Some of the fractures and crevices in the rock held pockets of water. It was a perfect habitat for certain creatures to flourish. However horses were not on that list, and I was relieved when we made our way past this black volcanic place.

When the roadside right of way returned to normal prairie Helen jumped back on Peter Pony and rode alongside the wagon. Today she rode bareback. Her short blonde hair blowing in the summer breeze, sitting straight and tall on her beloved pony. Together they jumped small washes and rode around the sharp yucca, past gopher holes, splashed through the sand and tiptoed over the rocks. She was in six-year-old cowgirl heaven. She and her pony were one. The highway we were traveling had very few cars using it. This was an isolated and desolate place. People in the cars usually waved as they passed. It was getting late in the morning and I was beginning to look for a level place off the highway to park for lunch. A car pulled up beside me and slowed to our pace. The passenger window was rolled down and out of it came a large plain white bag. I was bewildered at first as to why these people were handing me their trash. Upon inspection of the bags contents, I saw that it was contained four large hamburgers and French fries. I then thanked the lady profusely, and asked if we could pay for them. She waved me off and said she thought we would enjoy them, then drove away. I never even had the chance to ask her name. Angels are like that.

I dispersed a burger to the little cowgirl on her pony and she ate as she rode along. We all did. Becky sat on the wagon seat with me and we shared lunch while watching the four horses easily pull the wagon down the long straight highway to the west. Becky handed me the Polaroid camera and I took a picture of Helen eating her delicious hamburger as she trotted along on Peter Pony.

Figure 7. Lunch on the trail riding Peter Pony.

To the south of us was the White Sands Missile Range. It extended for miles and miles across the sagebrush dotted country. On the south end it turned into a sea of brilliant white sand for which it was named. It was because of this natural barrier, we chose to use the northern route we were now traveling.

The distance between towns this time, and water, was over forty miles. The next stop on the map was a place called Bingham. And that's exactly what it was, a place, and not a town. We made it in less than three days. Our water was gone when we parked in front of a property with a sign out front advertising 'Rattlesnake Pit'. That's all there was to Bingham. Population two. Not counting the den of vipers. To add to the ambiance of this was the fact that we were now just a mere fifteen miles north of the test site of America's first Atomic bomb. This information was relayed to us by the owners of the snake pit, Jones and his wife Vera. This is marvelous I thought. Rattlesnakes and atomic bombs. We should stay a few days. So we did. Mostly because Karen and Lee showed up again, and took us on a side journey in their truck to a place called Gran Quivira. It was an old Spaniard and Indian settlement from over 400 years ago. It was interesting, rich with history, and a refreshing side trip away from the daily routine of traveling at four miles per hour.

Rattlesnake Jones was gracious enough to keep an eye on our livestock while we were gone that day, but I was still anxious to get back to the horses and make sure all was well. Karen and Lee slept next to the wagon in their bedrolls that night. Just as the morning began to gray, the howling of coyotes awakened us. Lee called one in close by making a squeaking noise, and the girls stared in amazement at the sight a wild coyote just twenty feet or so away from the wagon. It looked at the bedrolls where the noise was coming from with great curiosity. Then turned and ran back into the sagebrush and sand.

That morning Rattlesnake Jones gave us all a free tour of his snake pit, and a brief history of rattlesnakes. We were informed that there were close to 28 species of rattler in America, and New Mexico was home to nearly half of those. Jones enjoyed crawling into rock out-crops and dens to search for rattlers for his pit. Because he was still standing there and owned a pit full of snakes, I presumed he was fairly good at what he did. In the center of the largest pit, a dead tree had been planted. Jones told us that after a cold night, the snakes would crawl up into the tree so as to be able to reach the suns rays in the morning. They would be hanging off each the trees branches like giant forkfuls of rattlesnake spaghetti, glistening in the morning sun. Proof that rattlesnakes can and do climb trees. Jones also told us that he found it necessary to trim one of the branches back a few feet because it was within four feet of the top of the pit. The snakes layered themselves onto it so that they created a bridge to the rim of the pit and had a successful jailbreak. He assured us that it had happened some time ago, and we had nothing to fear.

Figure 8. "Rattlesnake Jones."
(Image Courtesy of Gwen Jones-Poe and Cliff Coles, ©1988)

The pit itself was about twenty feet wide and just as deep. A short chain link fence surrounded the hole, so that small children, their parents and pets would not accidentally fall in. The rattlesnakes dined on rabbits supplied by their caretaker. Jones told us that on one occasion a large rattler seized the rabbit on one end, and a slightly smaller rattler started to devour the other. The snakes met in the middle, with half a rabbit down each of their gullets. The theory that snakes cannot disgorge was proven false, as the smaller snake released his meal to the larger. Our wagon trip was turning out to be quite an educational experience. These are things you just don't learn in school.

Karen and Lee left later that day and promised to catch up with us again. The next morning found us back on Highway 380 heading west. Late that day we crossed the Rio Grande River at San Antonio. We stopped on the far side and camped near the river. From there we paralleled I-25 north on a frontage road to Soccorro. There we bought two small bales of hay for leaner times. The road leading up into the mountains of Magdalena was nothing compared to the long hard pull we experienced leaving Roswell. We had camped at the base of the hill and all horses began the climb fresh from the evenings rest. The four horses easily managed the incline.

The same night I got little rest. It was the first and only time while camping alongside the highway that I felt insecure. We had a suitable shelter from the elements, just as long as a freak wind didn't blow the wagon over. But it wasn't bad weather that concerned me that night. It was the lack of security from persons with treachery in their hearts. Our Dutch door had no lock. Just a hole where a doorknob should have been. Anyone could have walked right in. Our only weapons were the stolen arrows from the church camp. We didn't even have a bow. Perhaps we could have poked an unwelcome burglar. It was our only form of home defense. The cause for my concern came from a car that cruised by slowly back and forth, very late at night, with its drunken inhabitants hollering obscenities at our campsite. I did not know what their intentions were, but I prayed they would not stop to bother the livestock or us. Eventually they grew bored and left. Had there been a problem, we would have no way to call for police. We were isolated and that was our usual scenario when we camped. I would keep the arrows handy.

At the top of the mountain was the town of Magdalena. At least I think that's what the few buildings I saw there represented. A Laundromat, a bar, and a tiny market. We stopped at the market for provisions. The same milk, ice, tortillas, refried beans and cheese that was our normal fare. We were good to go.

The Plains of San Augustine were a surreal sight. This flat bowl surrounded by mountains was carpeted with pale green gamma grass, nearly two feet tall. And growing out of this sea of green were miles of giant white disks pointed towards the sky. We were walking through the VLA project. Very Large Array. There were 29 enormous white satellite dishes dwarfing our wagon, neatly lined out in different directions across the plain. Like a tiny red ladybug we crawled through this valley of giant toadstools. Railroad tracks crossed the center of the valley floor but there was no train. The dishes were on rails, so that they could be moved along the tracks to any position needed. All twenty-nine focused on the same spot in the sky like a flock of chickens studying a bird of prey flying high overhead. Something was of interest to them, but whatever it was, we couldn't see it. We were earth bound. Searching for our evening's campsite where the horses could feast on the nutritious gamma grass.

Datil was a good two days walk from Magdalena. I had come to find out that just because there was a town noted on a map it did not necessarily mean there would be a grocery there. We never seemed to be able to store much food, due to the lack of money or the perishable properties of items that needed to be refrigerated. Our normal condition was that we had little money to buy food when it was available, or when a few dollars came into our hands, a market could be a day or two or three away.

Up to this point we always seemed to have something to eat, but the time was coming when that would not always be the case. To say that when we began this trip we stepped out on faith would be a lie. I didn't believe in God. Actually I didn't believe in a God that would allow me to go through all the horrible things my marriage had brought me. I was angry with God and we weren't speaking. Very angry. As I look back on this journey, I can now see that His hand was on me from the beginning. Like the blinder bridles that Dusty and Dolly wore, I was not able to see anything except what was in front of me. However, Dusty and Dolly, unlike me, had faith in that unseen person that was directing their steps at the end of their lines. They knew I was there, they could feel my presence. We communicated not by sight, but by slight messages sent down those lines. They could have chosen not to listen, and take the bit in their teeth to run their own direction, but in obedience and submission, they waited for my direction. I, on the other hand, chose not to communicate with my eternal guide. I was in rebellion, and angry, and fought the bit. And because of that, was going the wrong direction. My horses were smarter that I was.

The town of Datil represented the highest elevation of any we had come to on this trip. We were at seven thousand five hundred feet. It was late summer and the quaint town spoke of the harsh winters it had endured. Steep roofs on the houses to cast off excess snow were the norm. Large pines and spruce were scattered among its homes. Some of the houses were made of logs. It was very picturesque. We stopped for a few supplies and found a beautiful meadow beyond the town to camp at that evening. This was the high country. Elk could be heard bugling in the forest. That night we huddled under extra blankets to keep warm. As pretty as it was, I was anxious to move towards lower elevations in the event that an early snow would catch us unprepared.

Pie Town was the next spot on the map. It sounded like a great place to eat, but in fact the only thing open for business was an ancient two-pump gas station. Very disappointing. Gasoline was not one of the items we had needed for the last seven hundred miles. Not that we, a family of four, could have gone into a restaurant and bought a whole pie to eat. It was just the thought of something baked in an oven would be a real treat. The daily tortillas and beans or one-skillet dinners were getting old. We might have been able to buy a single slice and split it four ways, but Pie Town had no pies.

Figure 9. Lunch stop near Pie Town, New Mexico.

A few miles out of Pie Town a green highway sign appeared in the distance on the right hand side of the road. It was small for a highway sign. More like a sign for an approaching intersection to let you know what the upcoming street name was. There was no indication of any crossroad ahead. We were out in the middle of nowhere. The road was nearly level with just a slight slope falling away to the west and to the east of the sign. Upon closer scrutiny I could make out the words. 'Continental Divide'. I pulled the horses to a stop near the sign and we took a photo of the wagon next to it. Reaching and crossing the Continental Divide was quite a landmark. Yes, indeed, it was all downhill from here! But it was anything but downhill. We had nothing in front of us but the unending up and down through the mountains of New Mexico and Arizona.

As we finished staking out the horses that evening, an old station wagon rolled onto the grass behind us. A tall lanky gentleman got out of the car and introduced himself. He lived somewhere in the vicinity, further out in the hills. He said he was a holistic doctor and just wanted to stop and meet with us. Most folks are curious that way but few took the time to stop and get acquainted. I was certainly glad this man did. I wasn't sure what a 'holistic' doctor was, but I wanted to get his opinion if he'd give it, on Dusty's never ending seeping fistula. She had suffered with this nasty oozing hole in her neck since Texas. Could he help? I had tried everything, and there was no improvement. He looked at the gooey mess and said he'd send some concoction to us that he'd used on his dog's broken leg. Apparently, the leg had turned gangrenes and he said this potent stuff knocked the gangrene right out. I wasn't holding my breath, but if he'd get it to us, I'd try it. He assured me it would knock out the infection, or burn a hole down through her neck so that it could drain. I certainly hoped so. Nothing else I had available was changing a thing.

As we were continuing down the road towards the community of Quemado below, a small green car pulled into a turnout in front of us and parked. In it was a family we had known from when we had lived in Arizona. We had been in communication with them and they were anxiously awaiting our arrival. It was their desire to obtain a wagon and team and travel along with us. We would be wintering at or near their home in Chino Valley, Arizona, while they built their wagon and secured their team. Then when spring arrived, we would depart together for places yet to be decided upon. Bill and Jody were a unique couple. Years ago they had chosen to be a part of group following the teachings of a yogi and practiced TM. They had taken a vow of poverty and were very successful at it. Bill never had a real job, and in that way he and Fourth Person had common ground. Bill and Jody were free spirits and thought that *our* new way of life was the bee's knees. They, along with their two children had driven for hours in their little car in hope of finding us. We camped for the night then and there. A passerby stopped and offered us his catch of trout that day from the Quemado Lake. Dinner had been delivered. We talked of the realities of wagon life with Bill and Jody while we ate. Afterwards the visiting couple and their children spent a half-hour in meditation, humming their mantras, with their legs crossed, sitting in the dirt next to the wagon. They did this twice a day. Bill said if you kept at it long enough, you would learn to levitate. Like I stated, they were a unique couple.

Bill and Jody spent the next day with us. Helen and Becky enjoyed having other children to play with, and they explored the area around the campsite. Bill told us of his plans to use a stripped car chassis as a frame for his wagon. There was a dead vehicle abandoned in his back yard already. I questioned the unnecessary weight of such a frame, and told him of our troubles pulling some of the steeper hills. He informed us that the burros he planned to buy would powerful enough to do the job. Burros, I thought? You're going to use burros? I had a hard time with that concept. Bill had decided on burros because they were tough and only cost forty or fifty dollars each. That was in their budget. A team of horses would be way too expensive. And he had seen someone using burros to pull a wagon before. I dropped the subject. Spring was a long way off.

Jody and I drove their car west a few miles and stopped at the only grocery store in Quemado to stock up on a few items. We then went to a place along the highway further to the west a mile or so. Both sides of the highway grew abundant with a native plant called Navajo Tea.

We picked enough to stuff an empty feed bag full.

Figure 10. Navajo Tea Plant.

Back at the wagon, I fired up the black and sooty Coleman stove and boiled a pot of water. Jody cut up some of the Navajo Tea and threw it in. To my surprise, the roadside weed was delicious! The plant itself was tall, and spindly, growing two to three feet in height. It was gray green, stick like, with tiny yellow flowers and foliage that resembled toothpicks more than leaves. We had an endless supply of tea. I never ran across the plant anywhere else on our journey, but near Quemado it was abundant.

Bill and Jody left the next day to return home. We would be there in another month, and Bill needed to get their wagon finished, and find some burros. As I was going out to catch and harness the teams that morning, I managed to jam a sharp wooden splinter underneath the fingernail of my right pinkie. I pulled the splinter out and rinsed off the little blood that seeped out. Then proceeded to harness the big mares, and while doing so, cleaned and doctored Dusty's never ending wound. The next day I would regret that, as the infection found a home in the fresh puncture under my fingernail.

We rolled through the tiny place called Quemado, then stopped a few hundred yards past the last house on the right on the outskirts of the small community. Ray Baca walked over from the house and introduced himself. He was a Basque and lived there with his wife and mother. We were welcome to any water we needed.

A car slowed near us as we spoke with Ray, and an extended arm from the window passed us a baby food jar with a brown liquid in it. The unknown messenger was from the holistic doctor we had met a few days before. This was the medicine. It came with a recipe in case we need to make some more. The ingredients included myrrh and cayenne pepper, and a variety of other things. I took the brown liquid over to Dusty, cleaned out her wound again, and poured the jars contents into the infected pocket in the top of her neck. Had I known that my infected finger was going to become a serious problem, I would have saved some of the medicine back for myself.

We decided to stay here a couple of days to allow her to heal, if possible. Ray wanted us to ride out on his ranch with him, and that sounded like something we would enjoy, and besides there were no pending appointments we needed to be at. My finger started to throb that evening. The next day it was worse. Ray invited us into his home, where his gracious Spanish speaking wife gave me a bowl of hot water with Epsom salts to soak my finger in. As we sat at their dining table I could see a string of pus exiting from underneath my fingernail into the bowl of water. The pain was still getting worse. Dusty's wound however had changed over night. The dark pocket full of pus was now clean pink flesh. No more liquid oozed from the top of her neck. It was a miracle. By the end of the week the wound had nearly healed. The infection was gone. In a month the only sign left of the injury was a depressed spot at the place along her mane just in front of the withers.

Eventually her thick mane grew back and covered the spot completely. I however, was not faring as well. The painful finger was getting so intense that I could not sleep at night. I asked Ray if there was a doctor in town. The closest one was in Reserve, a town to the south. A call was made, and Ray and his wife drove me there to get my finger taken care of. My greatest fear was amputation. I liked my little finger, and would hate to see it go, but like a bad tooth, this pain had to stop.

The good doctor had me sit down on a stool in his examining room. I held forth my throbbing digit and watched with curiosity as the syringe needle entered beneath my fingernail. I could not differentiate the pain of the needle from the pain of the infection. And then the pain stopped. Ah. I watched closely as the doctor took a tiny pair of scissors and cut my fingernail from the tip to the base neatly up the middle. Then with a small pliers type tool, removed one side of the fingernail from my flesh, then the other. The bleeding was minimal. Betadine was applied, then an antibiotic ointment. The finger was wound with gauze until it was an inch in diameter, and I was good to go. No more pain. No more fingernail. I asked the doctor if the nail would grow back and he assured me it would, but perhaps not exactly as it had been before. He was right, and my nail returned very slowly. The cost for this procedure was eighty dollars. I had just enough to pay the bill. I left there with only three dollars in my pocket, but grateful.

When I walked back out into the waiting room, Ray's black eyes enlarged as he studied my enormous wrapped finger. "Did he have to cut it off?" he inquired. I assured him the finger was still intact, but the nail was now gone, and thanked them for the ride to get it tended to.

ARIZONA

The Arizona border was between Quemado and Springerville. It was hard to comprehend we had just walked across the state of New Mexico and half of Texas before that. A roadside sign announced our crossing. Beyond it the road stretched out into the horizon, flanked only by miles and miles of nothingness in all directions. Off on the horizon I could see the shape of a man walking. Just a tiny speck, but it was definitely a person walking alongside the opposite side of the road. I saw no sign of a stranded vehicle, so I assumed it might just be a local Indian working his way back home. The Zuni Reservation was not far away. As he approached I could see his facial features more clearly. Native-like, yet lighter complicated. Once we were abreast of each other I halted the teams and greeted the highwayman. He walked over to the wagon and introduced himself. His name was Hiyoshi Kono. He was Japanese and walking across the United States. He spoke English well and told us about his journey thus far. He had walked the length of Japan, went up to the Bering Strait. Kayaked down to British Columbia, and walked down into California. He was on his way to New York where he would hop a freighter to be dropped off in South America to walk that continent. I told him that we had traveled all the way from Texas. Whoopee do. It seemed like nothing compared to the world traveler standing there with us.

Hiyoshi pulled a Japanese flag out of his backpack. On it were the signatures of a half dozen or so people. Most were in languages I couldn't read. He wanted us to sign his flag. We were honored to do so. Then he reloaded the flag back into his pack and waved goodbye as he continued down the road in the direction we had just come from. I was humbled. In retrospect, I wonder if Hiyoshi finished his travels and wrote his story down in a book. I certainly hope so.

Springerville was the largest town we had been in since Roswell. We drove through and camped a few miles out of town. There was a little daylight left that evening, so I washed a few clothes and hung them out on the highway fence to dry. A person in a truck stopped to say a few words to Fourth Person while I was attaching a piece of laundry to the fence. I could hear the word 'squatters' mentioned and then the person drove away. Did that person really think we were squatters? We weren't planning on taking up residence on this highway easement. We had just camped there for one night. I'm sure they were delighted to see us gone the next day.

Vernon was the only place between Springerville and Show Low. We arrived there two days later. Camp was opposite an abandoned building. It was actually the only building in Vernon. We stayed there for one night, then continued on. It was mid September and early snowfall was a possibility. The nights were getting cooler. We were at a high elevation, traveling atop the Mogollon Rim. The pine trees grew thick and tall in places. Then opened onto mountain meadows. Cedar trees showed signs of strong winds, dwarfing and twisting them into grotesque shapes.

I was getting anxious to get into Show Low for our funds were getting very low. I hoped someone there would buy a picture, a pony ride or a drawing. At this point, a five-dollar bill would go a long way for this household. We walked into the town of Show Low at mid day. We were on the main four-lane street heading south through town along the business corridor. The horses were so accustomed to traffic by this time that semis passing within just a few feet of us did not bring a response from any of our four legged travelers. They just walked along. The only time on the entire trip that any of the horses spooked, was when Dusty spied a carousel horse stuck on a pole in the yard of a house we were passing. It must have looked like horse shish kabob to her, and she did her best to escape from the area as quickly as possible. But that was difficult for her to do because she was tied to a five thousand-pound wagon, and her teammate Dolly saw no reason to change gears. Dusty calmed down within a few hundred feet and assumed the steady pace of a well broke team.

I looked up when I heard tires squeal on the pavement. Then heard the subsequent metallic crunch. It came from across and down the highway. Someone in the opposite far lane a short ways down the road had rear-ended the car in front of them that had slowed to enter a parking lot. Thankfully it was just a minor fender bender. The parties involved were getting out to inspect the damage as we drove past heading the opposite direction. It was a case of someone not paying attention. I just prayed that it was not because their focus was on the big red wagon being pulled by four horses coming down the road. At any rate, I did not stop to ask, and we nonchalantly continued on our way. The only stop we made in Show Low was at a Circle K at the edge of town as we were leaving. No one had bought any cards, pictures, or pony rides, so the few dollars we had left were spent on milk and a bag of ice. We could go awhile on chocolate flavored milk.

We were many miles out of town when I spied a suitable campsite on the far side of the road. We would be able to pull quite a ways off the pavement. There was plenty of grass along the fence line, and what looked like a cattle tank with the possibility of water on the far side of the fence. So we parked, and went about unharnessing, unsaddling, watering and staking out our menagerie of nine horses and mules. Just as I tied out the last one, a Highway Patrol car pulled up. Officer Collison stepped out and told us we could not stay here, and that we would have to move. "Move? Move where? Why?" I asked. He didn't care, but we couldn't camp here. It was highway easement. Then he asked to see my driver's license. I told him I didn't have one, which I didn't. It wasn't necessary to have a driver's license to drive a team. When asked, Fourth Person said he didn't have one either. Officer Collison started to get frustrated with us. He growled, "What's your birthday?" to which Fourth Person answered "Why, are you going to send me a present?" Probably not the best reply, but for some reason we had already irritated the officer to the extreme. He said he would drive down the road and find a place for us to get off the highway and that we had better be moving when he returned. Had it not been for threat of having my girls removed from me had I been arrested, I would have dug in my heels and refused to comply. I knew we were not breaking any laws. By the time we were harnessed and back out on the road, it was nearly dark.

This was really dangerous. We were traveling at four miles per hour on a two-lane highway with a fifty five-mile per hour speed limit and we had no *lights*. The officer returned and told us there was a spot two miles down the road on the left that we were to go to. "Two miles?" I said. That would take us a good thirty minutes to reach, and we would be traveling in utter darkness before we made it. This was insane. The officer took a twelve inch square red flag out of the back of his cruiser and stuck it on the back of the large wagon. We had a slow moving vehicle sign larger than that on the back of the wagon already. I asked him if he really thought that a twelve inch square of cloth was going to be more visible than the ten foot tall bright red wagon it was attached to. Then I explained to the good officer that we had NO LIGHTS and were an accident ready to happen. He said that he would follow us to the campsite he chose for us. He dutifully pulled in behind us and for the next half-hour, crawled along behind us in the darkness with flashers on, at four miles per hour. I was livid. The lives of my girls and livestock were being threatened due to the lack of common sense of a man with a badge.

By the time I turned the team into the road leading off to the left, the officer had left to attend to more important matters. We drove along the last few hundred yards in darkness. There was a cattle guard in the road separating the highway from private land. We could not cross over it until the large sheets of plywood could be removed from the top of the wagon and placed upon the steel bars so that the horses could cross. That process took another ten minutes. There was no suitable campsite on the far side. This was all private land and fenced. We located a gate barely wide enough to drive the wagon through, and camped in someone's field. There was no water. It was late by the time we had unharnessed and staked the livestock out again. Feed was minimal. The local livestock had already grazed it down. We worked in total darkness. The girls had already gone to sleep. I didn't bother to wake them for a dinner of ramen soup and chocolate milk. They had cold cereal waiting for them a breakfast.

Daylight brought us our bearings. We had camped in a cow pasture that belonged to who knows whom. We weren't anxious to find out, so we harnessed up and got back out on the road in record time. With our luck the owner would have the same officer that told us to camp here arrest us for trespassing. Tonight I would scout for a spot off the highway, in the surrounding forest, to avoid another run in with Officer Collison. We saw him two days later. He waved as he drove by like an old friend.

Late that afternoon, I spied a small pond through the pines, and at the next Forest Service access road, put the team through the gate and followed the two track back into the forest. We were well hidden now. Shouldn't have to worry about anyone finding us a quarter mile off the highway on a road that dead-ended at this tiny pond. But I did worry about what we would be having for dinner. There was little left at the bottom of the Styrofoam chest. We had a quarter gallon of milk sitting in the last of the melted ice. A half stick of butter floated next to it. We had no canned goods. No bread. And no money. But that didn't matter because there were no stores. We were sitting in the middle of the Apache Sitgreaves National Forest miles from anyone. There would be no dinner tonight. Fourth Person decided at that moment to step up for the first time in eight years and provide for his family and walked out into the forest. He returned with a dead squirrel. From the looks of her, she either had babies, or was about to. I wasn't going to eat a mother squirrel. Fourth Person took the carcass and began skinning it. I couldn't watch. I was slipping into a depressed state, which I seldom did. My girls were going to have a half-cup of chocolate milk for dinner. I looked up through the pine trees into the sky beyond and tried to understand why God would allow my children to lack so much. No home, no beds to sleep in, no normal life, and now, no food.

I caught the flash of white from between the trees before I heard the engine. A car was coming up the road. Perfect! The sheriff had shown up just as Fourth Person was skinning a poached squirrel. But the car wasn't a car, it was a van, and it wasn't the sheriff. The van pulled up right next to the big red wagon and two men stepped out. "Hello" one hailed. "We thought you might like a couple packages of fresh tortillas!" Then they opened a side door on the van that read 'Arizona Brand Tortillas'. I almost cried. But instead thanked them profusely. We would be having warmed tortillas with butter this evening. Of course, there was the squirrel, but lacking onions and bell peppers, I would not be able to make 'Squirrel Fajitas.'

The men hopped back in their van and went on their way. It was almost dark. It was not possible for them to see us from the highway. I don't know how they knew to drive back on that road to our campsite, but I was grateful they did. As I look back on the incident now, there is no way you would ever convince me that God did not have a hand in that. He sent his messengers, like the ravens that fed Elijah.

After watering all the horses and mules at the tiny pond the next morning, we once again harnessed up and headed the teams west. The next real town was Payson, about 70 miles ahead. There were several smaller towns along the way that we could get groceries at, provided we made any money by the time we arrived at one. Just before the community of Overgaard a woman met us at her driveway where it connected to the highway we were traveling. She requested a pony ride for her daughter. It was the girl's birthday. I pulled the wagon over and Peter was saddled. Peter was led up and down the driveway several times. The girl was delighted. So was I. Her mother also bought some note cards. We proceeded down the highway with a five-dollar bill. At the next store I bought a loaf of bread, some lunchmeat, a quart of milk, and a can of refrieds. We were good for two days. I could stretch a five dollar bill a long way.

By the time we made it to Heber, we had enough extra change to use the Laundromat alongside the highway. I parked the teams and wagons in the large parking lot, then carried our dirty clothes in for a real wash with hot water. Clothes dried in dryers were not stiff like those hung on a barbed wire fence to dry. And they smelled nice, too.

We camped off the highway that evening once again. I was still concerned about being harassed by the local authorities. We had pulled off the highway into a grove of tall ponderosa pines and had just staked out the last horse when Bill and Jody drove up. I asked Jody how they tracked us down, and they said they looked for the road apples left by the horses. We were easy to track with nine horses and mules leaving their 'breadcrumbs' along the trail. We would be camped beyond the last pile left on the road.

The only thing I had to feed a group that large for dinner was dried beans I had just bought at the last town. The guys started a campfire and I put the beans on to soak and heat in a Dutch oven above the flames. This was my least favorite way to cook. The Coleman stove came in a close second. Hours later, long after dark, we dined on half cooked butter beans. Chewy on the outside and crunchy in the middle. Thank goodness for salt.

Bill and Jody said that they would come once a week and see how we were progressing. They camped in their car that evening, and we put all the kids together in the girls' bunk. It rained all night. The next day the sun had returned and we bid Bill and Jody farewell. The road turned south and pointed us towards the edge of the Mogollan Rim. It would be a long downhill drive into Christopher Creek.

We had been traveling parallel to the Mogollon Rim since entering Arizona. It stretched nearly two hundred miles across the state. On the top of this escarpment were ponderosa pines and mountain meadows. Below the rim's cliffs fell off into the desert high country. It is the wilderness written about in many of Zane Grey's western novels. We camped that evening near the rim. There is a beautiful meadow at the edge before the descent and in the center there was a pond. The deep grass for the horses was plentiful.

A couple pulling a travel trailer stopped near us. A woman came over to the wagon with a grocery bag full of food. She asked if I would mind taking it. She explained they were done with their camping trip and didn't want to take all the extra food home. They would just throw it out if I didn't want it. I accepted the leftovers eagerly. Inside were a variety of goodies we seldom bought. A full jar of peanut butter, bread, eggs, a package of cookies, lettuce, and bacon. Bacon! We hadn't had bacon since the Circle Six church camp. I cooked it up immediately. We all ate two slices each. What a treat! Within a half mile of our campsite the road turned west and hugged the edge of the Mogollan Rim as it dropped into the valley a thousand feet below. The slope was not steep and I was able to slow the wagon with the friction brake sufficiently as to ease the burden from the teams. All they had to do was walk, and all I had to do was keep the wagon from rolling over them. It took us an hour to reach the bottom. Ahead was the Christopher Creek Campground where we spent the night.

The campground had several other people staying there. All had motor homes or camp trailers. Several people came over to check us out and we sold some pictures and other items to them. I had taken some plain white plates and painted pictures of draft horses on them. Those were popular, and we sold one that evening for fifteen dollars. We would have some money to stock up on groceries when we reached the next town of Payson. It was two days away.

We were now traveling through the Arizona high country. The Tonto National Forest surrounded us for miles and miles on both sides of the highway. Tall ponderosa pines flanked the road. Smaller Pinion pines were scattered about along with manzanita, and scrub oak. The scent in the air was sweet with the scent of the pines and oak. We found a wide spot alongside the road where another road joined the main highway, and deemed it a good campsite for the evening. The area had been graded and was obviously used as a place to park off the highway. It was a dry camp, but we had enough water with us to satisfy everyone. Tomorrow we would be in Payson where I was confident we could get more. The horses were staked out once again, and I was going about the evening's chores. Helen and Becky had run off into the forest nearby to play.

A green U.S. Forest Service truck pulled up. Two men got out and told us we couldn't camp here. Oh no, not again, I thought. I pointed to the road turning off to the right and asked them if we could camp on the other side of the fence. They said no. That was National Forest, and you could only camp in designated areas. They also said the highway right of way was considered forest and we couldn't stay there either. I wished Officer Collison would show up so that they could argue about to whom the highway actually belonged. In the meantime, I explained that we would be gone in the morning. We were traveling by horse and there was no way that we could leave, now that it was nearly dark, and make it out of the Tonto National Forest Boundaries. We had to camp here tonight or on the other side of the fence if they preferred, but there wasn't much else we could do. We were just passing through, and because of our mode of transportation could not just turn a key and drive down the road. This information did not please them.

Then one of the men spied an ax that we had owned for years that was leaning up against the wagon. He held it up and said, "This is Forest Service issue!" and tossed it in the back of the green truck. I couldn't believe my eyes. He stole our ax! I was stunned. Is this what government employees do? The two men climbed back in their official green Forest Service truck and left with our ax and threat of coming back with the sheriff. We never saw them again. I was hoping that they *would* come back with the sheriff. I wanted to report a theft. We had done nothing wrong. We were not breaking any laws. Yet these Forest Circus people harassed us, threatened us with arrest and then stole our ax. I tried to comprehend the Gestapo tactics that I had just witnessed. Innocent of any wrongdoing I had been treated as a lawbreaker. It was upsetting that government employees could get away with such a thing. Later it occurred to me that our team harness was stamped 'U.S. Army'. I pondered the possibility of a passing convoy stopping and yanking the harness off the horses. From what I had just witnessed, anything was possible.

We escaped the boundaries of the National Forest the next afternoon. Payson was a welcome sight. We parked in an open field on the far side of town, just past a quaint shopping center that was built to resemble a Swiss village. We had refilled the horse water tank at a gas station, and purchased a few grocery items at a market along the highway.

The next morning we woke to overcast skies and the threat of rain. It was spitting light drizzle by the time we were out on the road. We were on Route 260, a two-lane highway heading west towards the towns of Pine and Strawberry. I kept the teams and wagon as far to the right as possible so as to allow traffic to pass without delay. The drizzle had turned into a rain. I started searching for a place to get off the highway. Any port in this storm would do. We crossed the bridge over the East Verde River and began to climb the winding road. The rain was coming down in sheets now. Visibility was low. Traffic was starting to back up behind us on the narrow road. A small pull out appeared ahead and I directed the team into the spot. It was barely long enough to contain us. The wagons were only five or six feet from the pavement edge. On the other side of the wagon was a sheer rock face of granite. I had parked the wagon so close to the vertical rock, that there was just enough room to step off the porch. It would have to do. We were squeezed between a rock and a highway. There was no place on this side of the road to tie out the stock, so we led them across the road to the far side to stake them out for the night between granite boulders and pinion pine trees. Grass was scarce. I hoped in vain that the storm would break and we could move on to a more suitable spot. It was early in the afternoon, but the skies were dark, and the rain was relentless. We were drenched to the skin by the time all the horses were secured. I was happy that the wagon kept the girls high and dry. A canvas top wagon would not have fared so well. I was grateful for the big red box. We were able to heat the wagon somewhat with the Coleman stove. Our living space was a mere one hundred twenty eight square feet. It didn't take much to warm it up. Wet clothing was hung to drip wherever a place was found. After putting on a dry set of clothing, we were snug and warm, and ready to ride out the storm.

A summer rainstorm in the Arizona high country normally lasted only an hour or two, if that. But this was different. This storm lasted non-stop for three days. We heard later that the storm had done much damage, and extreme flooding had isolated the towns of Clifton and Morenci to the south and east. As soon as it was daylight the second day we harnessed in the rain and drove on until we came to a better campsite. Thank goodness it was only three miles up the road. There we stayed until the rain finally quit. The harnesses were soaked. Nearly everything was wet. There was a small tarp on the little wagon under which we put the saddles and as much else as would fit. When the rain finally stopped, I spread around some of the rain soaked items to dry in the bright Arizona sun. It didn't take long.

The sun was shining and the birds were singing as we drove into the tiny town of Strawberry a few days later. Strawberry is a cute little mountain town, surrounded by tall pines and well kept homes. A local family we had met a few days earlier offered to give the horses a ride in their stock trailer, and pull the wagon the next few miles with their truck. Just outside of Strawberry the road led back up to the top of the Mogollan Rim. It was short but steep and I was concerned about how and if the horses could manage it. It took two trips with the large horse trailer to haul the horses to the top. Then they hooked onto the wagon and brought it up. We regrouped at a large area off the main road at the top of the rim. Looking back down the steep road, I couldn't imagine how the horses would have climbed it. Once again, angels were there at just the right time. I thanked them profusely, and they drove away. In the midst of the tall Ponderosa pines where they had left us, Helen and Becky discovered a spring fed pond teeming with goldfish. The top of the pond glittered with flashes of red and white fish. Delighted with their find, Helen and Becky spent the remainder of the day trying to fish with empty coffee cans. The horses got the afternoon off.

Figure 11. Stopped along the General Crook Trail.

Bill and Jody arrived that day with family in tow, and camped for the night. All the children kept busy with their fishing and actually caught a few. They were of course drenched by the time that was accomplished. The captive fish went home with Bill and Jody the next day. For us, everything was downhill from here. At least until we reached Camp Verde.

The General Crook Trail led us from the pine-covered mountains into the high meadows above the Verde River. Camp that evening was in a sea of green grass. A cow tank across the highway held water for the horses. The lush grass was the most I had seen for quite awhile. The horses ate their fill that night. Fourth Person went into one of his violent tirades that afternoon. I seriously contemplated hitching a ride with the next passing car, but the thought of leaving the horses behind in his care quashed the thought.

The next day found us going down into the Verde Valley on a long stretch of road that seemed to drop continually, hour after hour. It must have been a six- percent grade or steeper. I rode the brake non-stop to keep the wagon off the horses. It allowed them the opportunity to spend the day just walking down the long road, with no weight to pull. On our right, the guardrail snaked along the canyon into the bottom somewhere below, separating us from the steep drop off on the far side. As we descended, I noticed evidence on the guardrail that a frantic trucker had been forced to use it to slow his rig down. Parts of it were smashed flat and the black rubber from his large tires had left their streak along it continually for several miles. I tried to imagine what conditions had happened to cause the loss of his brakes, and hoped I would not have to do the same. It was a long way down to the valley below. We did not make it to the bottom that day. Camp was on a mountainside overlooking Camp Verde.

The large pullout area I chose for camp that evening had an added bonus. Just across the highway fence was an empty holding pen belonging to a local rancher. And there was an access gate into it from the highway. It was less than an acre large, but we put several of the horses into it for the night. The grass wasn't thick, but sufficient, and the horses enjoyed the freedom. It was one of the few times along the trip they didn't have to spend the night tethered to a fifty foot rope.

We arrived in Camp Verde the next day. The town was familiar to us and I had the feeling I was getting close to home. Prescott was just over Mingus Mountain to the west. We would be delayed in Camp Verde for a week due to an invitation to stay at Rainbow Acres for their upcoming celebration. The country atmosphere of Rainbow Acres was home for retarded adults. They even had a horseback-riding program overseen by a woman named Trudy. We were asked to give wagon rides with the small wagon and in return, they would put us up for the week, horses and all. Such a deal. We accepted.

After settling in and caring for our horses, Trudy took us over to their stables and introduced us to their dude string. They were well cared for, fat, and each had their own small pen. Trudy told us that most of the horses there had been donated, and were very gentle and very well broke. They were good mounts for the special folks that lived there. They needed to be. They had to be safe. Their passengers were slow of mind and body. The horses they rode were also slow of mind and body. Most due to advanced age, but some due to old injuries, aches and pains. They were a good match for each other.

As we walked past a chain link enclosure, a gray mare charged us, barred her teeth and snapped the inside of the fence, popping it as she lunged toward us. Her ears were laid back flat and she had a mean look in her eye. She turned her butt towards us and feigned a kick. I looked at Trudy and asked, "What's her story?" Trudy said she had been donated, and was a registered Appaloosa mare, but

94 • MARILYN J. WILEY

because of her nasty disposition would never be a usable horse. For anyone, retarded or otherwise. They would have to find her a new home. Most likely on a boat going overseas to a country that dined on grain fed horse. She was a pretty mare standing a good fifteen hands tall. Her body was well built and balanced. Her coloring was nearly white. If she had a blaze or stockings you would not have been able to see them because her body coloring was so light. Her eyes however were dark. Partly with anger, but mostly a dark chocolate color, deep and empty. I knew there was a horse in there somewhere. I had very little money, certainly not enough to buy a horse. So I asked Trudy if they'd trade her for a used refrigerator and washing machine. She'd ask the owner.

Before we began the wagon trip, months before, the two appliances we owned were sent to Bill and Jody's with a relative. They could use them until whatever time came we needed them back. Time had come. We didn't need the appliances. An Appaloosa mare could be sold for more than the value of the washer and refrigerator. The deal was struck. We now owned a horse with a serious personality disorder.

One of the main reasons horses end up with problems is that like bored teenagers, they just don't have enough work to do everyday to stay occupied and out of trouble. We had a rolling boot camp for delinquent horses. Her mother never told her about people like us. There would be plenty of things to do, places to go, and things to see. I had no doubt she would turn into a well broke horse, with enough time and training. Her time had come. Smokey joined the Buffalo Chips and Company traveling circus. A year later Smokey was sold to a retarded girl. She had turned out to be one of the most patient, dependable, and calm horses we had ever owned.

The weekend before we left the Rainbow Acres Ranch brought in a balloonist to give residents and guests a tethered ride. Helen and Becky went up in the balloon and had delightful time. Two days later we harnessed up the teams and headed south on Interstate 17.

There were several roads leading out of the Verde Valley. All went up. The climb this time would be five or six miles long. There were no frontage roads through the pass. We would have to stay on the Interstate until we reached the turnoff to Dewey beyond the summit. It was only eight miles from Rainbow Acres to the base of the mountain. The horses would still be fairly rested from their weeklong reprieve. They would need their reserve strength. It was a long way up. Fourth Person rode Smokey that morning. Smokey was broke to the saddle. She never offered to buck but her steering was all messed up. The fact was she had no steering. She just went. It's a horse's nature to stay close to the herd. So she never lost sight of us. But she was all over the road, literally. Due to all the strange sights and sounds, including the wagon that she was not wanting to get close to, Fourth Person had his hands full. First she went this way, and then she went that way. She didn't know where she was going, but she didn't want to be late. Smokey ran backwards across the southbound lanes of Interstate 17 and ended up galloping down the median. Fourth Person was just along for the ride. Eventually he worked her back to the wagon, where she calmed down and decided to follow the herd. She was hot and sweaty and tired from her workout. And content to just walk along quietly for awhile. I'm sure she was wondering to herself, "How long could this last?" This was probably the longest ride, and only time she had traveled a whole eight miles in her life.

We pulled off the Interstate at General Crook Trail, the last exit at the base of the mountain. There we parked in a pull out where a road should have gone to the right at the stop sign. But there was no road, just a closed and locked gate. On the far side, a narrow dirt road dead-ended at a windmill about a quarter of a mile away. We would water the horses there. The locked gate would not deter us. We would only have to loosen the four strands of barbed wire and walk the horses across. The water tank on the small wagon had not been filled on purpose. Like a balloonist lightening the load, we cast off excess weight for the climb ahead. We would have to water the horses from the windmill.

That night Helen and Becky became sick with stomach flu. They tried to use the bucket I set out, but at times didn't make it. Their bedding was spotted with vomit. The next morning, I took the soiled blankets and placed them in large black plastic garbage bags. It would be a while before I would have water to wash them or could find a laundry. Thankfully, Helen and Becky were feeling better the next morning. As I began the morning chores tending the horses a car pulled up. In it was a familiar face. Two familiar faces. It was my mother and my Aunt Florence! They had driven over from Prescott Valley. Mom asked if they could take the girls home for a visit. We could pick them up in a few days on our way through to Chino Valley. Mom also said she'd be happy to do any laundry. I told her about the illness that had struck the girls the night before, and gave her the soiled blankets. Thank God for moms! Helen and Becky would enjoy a bathtub full of bubbles and have a real bed to sleep on. Grandma Genevieve also supplied ice cream cones and Grandpa Harold would whip up his delicious famous mashed potatoes for dinner. Helen and Becky could even watch television. It would be like a trip to Disneyland for them. I was delighted they could go. But there would be a price to pay.

Fourth Person did not like my parents. Actually, he didn't like most people. Once I witnessed him slap his own mother. Twice. Later when I questioned her about the incident, she said it was her fault. That she had provoked him. I wanted to tell her it was a good thing he didn't have a gun at the time. The outcome may have been far more serious.

Fourth Person had some issues. I'm sure it was due to his paranoid schizophrenic personality. But my girls were loaded into the car, and I was willing to accept the consequences. They needed a break, and a hot bath.

After the girls left, I kept busy harnessing the four horses and stayed away from Fourth Person as much as I could. We soon would be out on the highway, and he would be preoccupied with other things. I never harnessed the teams so quickly as that morning. By the time the extra animals were secured to the wagon, I was in the seat and clucked to the teams. We rolled back out onto the Interstate. Every step we took was uphill. The four horses handled it easily until the slope steepened. Fourth person tied onto the front of the tongue with the lariat and the new mare became the fifth horse pulling. This was a new job for her, but Smokey learned quickly. We had several miles of uphill to pull.

The Verde Valley was home for several colorful towns. Camp Verde was named after the old soldier fort there, Fort Verde. Jerome sat on the north slope of Mingus Mountain. It was an old copper mining town. Tourists and artists had infused the ghost town with new life and quaint little shops. Sedona and Oak Creek bordered the north. Their red rock cliffs and rock formations could be seen for miles. It had been the backdrop for many western movies. Cottonwood and Clarkdale butted up against each other near the center of the valley along the Verde River. Other small towns dotted the valley floor. Cornville, Rimrock, and others. The terrain varied continually. Pine trees, cottonwoods and cactus all had a home in the Verde Valley. The rock cliffs and surrounding mountains were shades of red, gray, white, green, and yellow. It was an interesting area rich with history.

Our goal this day was to escape the valley. The horses walked deliberately up the never ending slope, seeking the summit where they could rest. We were walking through a gap in the Mingus Mountain Range. On the far side of the highway you could still see the original General Crook Trail where horses, pack trains and wagons used to roll. The mountains went up almost vertically a thousand feet or more. They were covered with scrub oaks, yuccas, dark volcanic rock and wisps of yellow grass. About half way up the climb, a large pullout appeared on the right. I pulled in to let the horses breathe. The five pulling together made a big difference. The weight was divided easily between the group, but it was still an uphill climb. Dolly was not gasping like she had that one time back in New Mexico, but this was still a workout, and she was an old horse. I let her rest till her breathing was normal.

To the right of us was a small narrow side canyon leading off towards the west. I could see small caves dug into natural outcroppings. Curious, I went over to inspect their depth, only to spook a pair of javalinas from their mid day nap inside. They grunted and ran along a narrow trail back up into the canyon wilderness. The hair on their back end lifted up in warning as they ran. Javalinas were introduced into Arizona many years ago. They are a pig-like creature, complete with snout. Also known as collared peccaries. Unlike a feral hog, they don't get very large. Some say they're not related to a pig at all. They are totally covered with prickly hair and it seems as though their head is half the size of their body. Like feral pigs, they sport large white canines and they're not afraid to use them. Fortunately, they have poor eyesight and had difficulty focusing on a stationary target. They tend more to follow their nose.

When I jumped back up on the wagon, all the horses were ready to go. The hardest part of the climb was still ahead of us. We had a couple miles to go. Traffic on the Interstate was normal. Semi trucks passed us groaning under their loads and grabbing lower gears. On the north bound lanes an emergency runaway truck ramp filled the median. The tracks of a large truck indented the loose gravel one third the way along the ramp. It had been there at the right time for someone. The road down into the Verde Valley was a bit steeper than the one climbing out was. And it was steep enough. As we came around a bend in the road I could see the summit ahead. It had been two hours since we left that morning's camp at the bottom of the hill. I pulled the horses into the turnout at the summit and let them rest. The view behind us was breathtaking. The valley spread out below had a green streak running through this end of it marking the course of the Verde River. Beyond you could see the red and white cliffs of the Sedona area. Beyond that, many miles away were the snowed covered volcanic cones of the San Francisco Peaks near Flagstaff. The sky was cerulean blue. White popcorn clouds dotted the sky. It was hard to comprehend all that was laid out in the vista before me. I was mesmerized by the immensity of it. Fourth Person rode over and insisted we move on. He intended to get Helen and Becky back as soon as possible. We would make the three-day trip in two.

A few miles down the Interstate, we turned west on the road to Dewey, Arizona. My focus turned once again to finding water. I would stop at the first place possible. It had been a hard pull for the horses and though we had not covered many miles, it had been hard work. They needed water. A few miles after turning west I spied a windmill to the right. There was a chain link gate leading from the highway to the road that led to it. I pulled the wagon off to the side of the road. We led the horses the quarter of a mile in to the windmill. A concrete rectangular tank held water from the continually spurting pipe. Because it had taken so long to lead all the horses down to the water, I convinced fourth person to camp for the night and let the horse's rest. It was another ten miles into Dewey, and another eight to my parent's home in Prescott Valley. We could do the full eighteen miles the next day.

We rolled into the gravel parking area of the Blue Hills Market the next day around noon. Parked across from us was a Holsom Bread delivery truck. The driver looked familiar. It was a person I had known from my previous home in Chino Valley. He recognized me and came over to talk. Many years ago his daughters had been in a 4H club I was a member of. I told him about the trip. The look on his face was that of disbelief. He then said he'd tell his daughters I said hello and went his truck. When he walked back he carried several loaves of day old bread and handed them to me. I thanked him. We would make sandwiches for lunch.

There were eight miles still between us and my parent's home in Prescott Valley. It would take two hours to get there. Mom and Dad had built one of the first homes in the area. They did nearly all the work themselves. Although there was a large open field in front of their home, Fourth Person, wanting to distance himself chose a spot down the road. It was a short walk to my parent's home. I was happy to see my girls sparkling when I walked in the door. Mom and Dad were hurt that we could not stay for the dinner they had prepared for us. Fourth Person made an excuse to leave immediately, taking the girls and me with him. I just looked at them, apologizing with my eyes for his rude behavior. I know Mom and Dad had been sick with worry about the trip that we had just made. To their credit, they did not make it harder on me by adding feelings of guilt and despair. Fourth Person hustled the girls out the door. I told Mom and Dad goodbye and said we'd be heading out in the morning to Chino Valley to meet up with Bill and Jody. I knew their hearts were breaking but I was trapped. They knew it. I knew it. No words were needed. All they could do was keep me in their prayers. It was not the horses, nor the mode of travel that caused their grief. It was the person I was married to.

The next morning we left earlier than usual and went north through Prescott Valley on Robert Road. It dead-ended at Highway 89A. There we turned west again and followed it towards Highway 89. We camped that evening on the east side of the abandoned railroad tracks, close to Granite Creek. This area felt very familiar to me. I felt like I was finally home. We had one more short day of travel left. This portion of our journey was nearly at an end. We would spend the winter with Bill and Jody while they finished their wagon, then head out in the spring to who knows where. We had been on the road with the team and wagon since April. It was October. I leafed through the daily journal I had been keeping and counted up the actual days we were walking down the road. It had been seventy-eight days. Tomorrow would be seventy-nine. Our home for the last six months had been an eight-foot by eighteen-foot box, pulled by horses across three states. I couldn't comprehend it. It hadn't seemed that difficult. Yet it was remarkable. I had no idea at the time that this would be my home for yet another year, and our journey was far from being over.

The next day, we drove the last ten or twelve miles to Bill and Jody's home in Chino Valley. As we rolled north along Highway 89 a small truck passed us and then stopped. Out hopped Bruce Hurley. He had been a friend of ours when we lived in Chino Valley many years before. He was a tall and lanky and always fun to be with. Bruce was the youngest boy in a family of thirteen. His older brothers Leo and Paul always told stories of how they pestered their little brother while growing up. Theirs was a large family filled with many adventures. Bruce visited for a few minutes and then drove away. His stopping to say hello had brightened my day. He was the first of many people we knew that would stop to greet us.

I had mixed feelings as we drove through Chino Valley. There were many places here that were familiar to me.

Places where friends used to live. Places I had ridden Rocky to and from. The ranch where I had bought him. Roads that led down to homes where I had lived. Stores where I had shopped. In the bright red wagon I drove down the main street in my own private homecoming parade. At the far end of town after traveling so many hundreds of miles west, we headed east. A mile and a half down Perkinsville Road we pulled in to Bill and Jody's home and parked the wagon. The horses could rest now. Behind the home was an abandoned pasture owned by the town. It was fenced and hadn't been grazed for years. The horses would have plenty to eat. No one cared if they were out there. The grass was tall from years of neglect, and dry now from the long summer. The horses didn't care. They could rest and eat through the winter.

Between where the wagon was parked and the back door of Bill and Jody's trailer, was the car frame Bill was working on. From the time he told us about till now it didn't look like any more progress had been made. There were two axles with the original car tires and the frame that held it together. It looked even heavier than I imagined. It was narrow. I was wondering how much room their family of four would have when a box was built on top of it for shelter. Bill had acquired three burros. They were pastured at his mother's place in Skull Valley. Bill said none of them were broke yet. They barely were broke to lead. And he also said that they were hard to catch. I volunteered to help them start the burro training when the time came.

I had never been inside the doublewide trailer that Bill and Jody owned. It looked like it was way overdue for a fresh coat of paint on the outside. It was a dreary green color and sat flush with the ground. The first time I went in it took a few minutes for my eyes to adjust to the darkness. All the windows were covered with heavy drapes so that very little light came in. There was no porch at either entrance. You just stepped from the dirt across the threshold. I found myself standing in what should have been the kitchen. What identified the room was an old refrigerator. There was no sign of a stove or sink. Those were buried under an enormous heap of dirty pots and pans, dishes, paper plates, bags of half eaten tortilla chips, egg cartons, towels, candles, paper of all variety, open cereal boxes, plastic bags, glasses, bowls, toys, shoe boxes, lamps, rope, magazines and old bread. The floor crunched under my feet as a made my way to the next room. There the dining table held the excess of what wouldn't fit in the kitchen. Boxes of clothing, shoes, more magazines, car parts, and other unidentifiable objects surrounded the floor perimeters. I made my way through the living room to the bathroom. The dreary green paint from the outside of the trailer had found its way onto the walls inside. It nearly matched the olive green of the stained toilet with no tank lid, and the small bathtub that was now home to a transmission and other amputated auto parts. Across from the bathroom was the main bedroom. In it was a king size mattress and box spring lying on the floor. It nearly filled the whole room. So much so that the door into the room would only open half way before it hit the bed. A pile of blankets lay crumpled across it. Pillows of many shapes and sizes and colors were scattered over the top and around the sides. When you stepped into this room you stepped up onto the bed. There was no place else to walk. On the far side of the bedroom was a closet full of more boxes, overstuffed, spilling their treasures out onto the bed and floor on the far side. Clothing was piled several feet high along the closest wall. This was where Bill and Jody and both children slept, all sharing the same bed. There was a second bedroom, but Bill's many art projects took it up. It had the feel of a cramped basement with only a tiny light focused on a worktable to warm the darkness. A radio tuned to a rock and roll station played continually. I was starting to have misgivings about this family that wanted to join our wagon tour. Their lifestyle was too similar to that of my spouse's family. The one I had just fled from.

Jody cleared a burner on the stove. Washed a pot and filled it with canned refried beans. Dinner was on its way. Small round corn tortillas were then heated in grease on the same burner. Apparently the only one that worked. Or perhaps it was just too much trouble to find the other three. That would be my guess. The greasy tortillas were smeared with the heated beans, and topped with grated cheese. Dinner was served on a paper towel. "Eat all you want "Jody announced. "We've got plenty!" They certainly did. This was the food of choice for lunch and dinner—every single day. During our two-month stay here, hot dogs crossed the menu one time. I think it was a holiday. And up until now, I thought our boring menu was bad. We sat down on an old broken down sofa to feast on our tacos. Between my boots, a ten-inch long centipede appeared from under the sofa and slithered across the dirty carpet. It was gone in a flash into a pile of boxes and clothing on the far side of the room. I quickly finished the last bite of my taco and took the girls outside to play. It terrified me just to think of what else might be lurking in and under Bill and Jody's possessions. Mice had taken over the cupboards and closets. I had to work on turning a blind eye to the filth these people lived in. Fortunately, I had many years of practice with my spouse's family. They were cut from the same cloth. Pigskin.

Our original plan was to stay here until Bill had his wagon ready to roll. From the looks of it not much had changed over the summer. And during the eight weeks or so we were there it was never touched. There was another small wagon in Bill's yard. It belonged to us. We had sent it ahead to be stored with the refrigerator and washer. It would be too small for a family to live in. It was identical in shape to the one we pulled behind us on the day we left. Only this one was smaller. The box was painted green and it had orange painted wooden wheels. A single horse could pull it easily. We made arrangements with a local stable to trade it for another horse, thinking that it would be easier to sell a horse than an old wooden wagon.

The stable owner delivered a small dark red sorrel mare in exchange for the wagon. She was only about thirteen hands tall. Closer to the size of a pony than a horse. She was about three or four years old. She had been handled a lot, but never saddled. As soon as she had completed her training with Buffalo Chips and Company's 'affirmative action' program, she would make a great mount for a youngster. Becky named her Cinderella. I thought the name fit perfectly. After a few weeks living with us she would be looking for a Prince to rescue her. The small amount of cash we had was quickly diminished. We needed some income. It wasn't likely that Fourth Person would find employment over the winter. It wasn't likely he would even look. When the local high school announced they were hosting a Christmas arts and crafts show I signed up for a space. I gathered up a bag of dry, smooth, wild gourds along the roadside that were common to the area. After wiping them off I painted them with a white base coat then decorated them with southwest designs and running horses. Then poked a piece of baling wire into the top and formed a loop. They made a pretty tree ornament. I painted several dozen. Then took them along with my rattlesnake buckles, leather wallets, painted plates and drawings to the craft show. There was a good crowd and I sold a surprising amount of items. Many of the locals recognized me from the time years ago when I had called Chino Valley home. It was good to see some old friends. The money made that day went to put in a small supply of food and Coleman fuel.

Winter arrived. One morning we awoke in the wagon to see a blanket of snow a few inches thick covering the landscape. Both burners of the Coleman stove were turned on and soon the one hundred twenty eight square feet of wagon was warm. I preferred the smell of Coleman fuel in the wagon to the smell of the never-ending bubbling grease used to make the daily tacos in the house. Most of my time was spent outside with the horses or in the wagon. As with most winter storms in Arizona, they don't last long, and in a few hours, or days, the snow would be gone and dust would again rise from vehicles passing on the dirt roads nearby. On a few occasions we harnessed up the old stud and Buttons to the small water wagon. We would use it to drive to the local market when necessary. Most of the roads in Chino Valley were just dirt and maintained by the city's road grader. We were a big hit with the kids on their way to school and offered rides to the ones we met walking down the road.

By mid December it was obvious Bill was not concerned about getting a wagon built in a timely fashion. There was always something more important he needed to get done. Meditating took a bite out of his day on both ends. And although Bill could talk all day about the history of a hammer I don't believe he knew which end was used to drive a nail. He finally suggested we all head on down to Skull Valley where he could work with his burros and we could all get out of the colder climate. That sounded good to me. There was a green pasture waiting for us that his mother owned. It would feel good to get back on the road again. If only for the two days it would take to walk there.

The morning we left, the local Prescott paper showed up for pictures and a story. Then we passed the local television station just off of Willow Creek Road and were interviewed again. Just outside of Prescott we camped for the night on Iron Springs Road. We were surrounded by pine trees, granite boulders, and oak brush. There was little grazing available, but the horses had fattened a little in Chino, and they would have good pasture again the next day.

Fifteen miles away was the community of Skull Valley. The legends around this place said that the valley floor was once littered with bleached bones. The remnants found by early pioneers of a fierce battle between the tribes of apaches that lived there. The valley has a creek running through it. You could tell where the creek was by the enormous cottonwood trees that grew along its edge. The bases of some of these ancient trees were almost ten feet across. As we entered the valley floor, we passed beneath a railroad known as the Pea Vine. It wiggled its way up from the main railway in the desert below, into the central mountains and on to Flagstaff. Here it went right up the center of the valley. The downtown area consisted of the Skull Valley General Store, an old two-pump gas station and a tiny restaurant.

Figure 12. On Perkinsville Road leaving Chino Valley, Arizona.

We crossed back over the railroad tracks at the store and turned left. Less than a mile up the road we turned right into a driveway and parked in an open grassy area. There was a house to our right and a bunkhouse looking structure across from us. A woman came from the house and greeted us cordially. She didn't look happy. It was Bill's mother. I asked her if we were okay to park in that place or if there was another she preferred. Most likely she preferred we were in another town but instead said that we were okay where we were. Bill and Jody came out of the bunkhouse as Bill's mother retreated to her home. Bill and Jody gave us the tour of the property after the horses were unharnessed and put in the small pasture. The burros were there and came up to the fence, curious as to whom it was that had invaded their territory. It was nice to be down below the snow line. It was not as cold here. The grass was already turning green under the trees. The horses had plenty to eat. We, however, did not. I was concerned about running out of food. As pretty as Skull Valley was, there was no source of income for us here. We didn't need much, but we did need some. Provisions were getting low. There was a small store a half-mile away but our money had run low. Very low. We had less than ten dollars to feed this family of four. Making it stretch was going to be a challenge. We were stuck here until Bill got his wagon ready. I offered to start training the burros but Bill insisted on doing it by himself. The days passed and they were never taken out of the pasture. I'm not sure what Bill was doing between his meditation times, but the unfinished wagon and burros remained right where they were when we rolled in.

I spent the days working with Helen and Becky, teaching them to read, and helping them with some workbooks. They loved the Word Bird series. Both became avid readers. I enjoyed reading the girls stories, and we colored in their coloring books.

The days dragged on with no sign of preparation by either Bill or Jody. The skies were gray from winter storms that left snow in the higher elevations. The worst we got was rain. But even that was depressing. I felt trapped. Our food was nearly gone. Our money was nearly gone. My hope had been replaced by depression. And that took some doing. It wasn't my nature to get depressed. We had walked over a thousand miles to come here. This had been our destination. To meet up with friends and travel together. We had no other destination. We had no goals. I was despondent, frustrated, broken.

A couple of weeks after arriving, a neighbor lady came over and asked me if I would mind helping her butcher some chickens. "I'd be happy to", I replied. And spent the next day plucking feathers from her flock of hens. As she would bring the freshly decapitated birds into the kitchen, I would soak them in a bucket of hot water and pull the feathers. While I did that, she would open the birds up and pull out unlaid eggs, entrails and organs. I was hoping that my labors would be paid for with one of the dead birds to take back and fry up for my family. Our cupboard was getting very empty. But that evening I walked back to the wagon with no chickens. Not even an egg. Just a 'thank you' as I walked out the door. I sunk into despair.

The next morning I walked down to the store, counted out the change in my pocket and bought a package of tortillas and a small chunk of cheese. When this was gone, it was up to God. Then I walked back to the wagon. Becky was inside crying over a mark on her hand. Bill's son had bit her. She had been swinging on the swing set and he wanted her seat. When I told Bill about it his reply was "It's his only defense against her!" I went back to the wagon. Then told the family, "We're leaving in the morning." Bill's burros had not been handled since we had arrived. No work had been done on Bill's wagon. We needed to be on our way before it was our bones scattered across the valley floor. That night we decided to head towards Phoenix. Fourth Person's grandmother lived there. We *needed* a goal. That was it. Then, from there, who knows where?

Early in the morning we caught up the horses. They were fresh from their rest and as anxious to get out on the highway as I was. We filled the water tank in the back wagon with water, and then noticed one of the tires had gone flat. We had no way to air it up. It had been fine the day before. My suspicion was that Bill had maliciously let the air out sometime during the night, angry that we were leaving. We needed the water. It wouldn't be prudent to dump it. An air hose could be had at the tiny gas station a half mile down the road. So we left pulling the small wagon with its flat tire, hoping that it had enough air left in it to make it to the station. It did. And it held. There was no leak. The air that had escaped had been helped.

From Skull Valley, we drove towards Kirkland. We had barely gone a few miles when a cement truck pulled ahead of us and stopped near a giant cottonwood tree. The driver crawled down out of the cab and hailed us to pull in behind and stop. It was Dan, Fourth Person's younger brother. What an encouraging sight. This was the man that had been in Carlton, Texas the day we left. He had handed us thirty-six dollars as we departed on our journey almost a year ago. Since then, he had moved his family to Prescott, Arizona, and had taken a job driving a cement truck. Dan asked if Becky and Helen could ride with him on his delivery. There was a bag of potato chips on the seat of the truck. The girls scrambled up into the seat and seriously damaged the bag's contents. Dan said he'd buy the girls lunch and bring them back later in the day. His generosity was equal only to my thankfulness. Then he handed us a few dollars from his wallet, just as he had done almost a year before a thousand miles away.

Dan pulled the huge cement truck back out on the highway and we continued towards Kirkland. We were on a narrow two-lane country road. There was no shoulder to drive on. The traffic on this road was light and the few cars that traveled on it passed us easily. To our right was the Pea

Vine railroad tracks. There had been no train that morning. We made it to Kirkland and drove past the only building in town, the Kirkland Bar. In its heyday, the two story stone building had been a stage stop, housing the same bar, a hotel and brothel. Just past the bar the road ended at a T. To the right across the railroad tracks was the road that led to Hillside, and Bagdad, an old copper mining town. It also connected to a road leading to Congress, a place we would need to pass through on our way to Phoenix. But I was not familiar with that road, except that it was dirt, crossing through open range and most likely pocketed with cattle guards. To our left was the continuance of the road we had been on. It went to Peeples Valley and Yarnell where the closest market was located, two days hence. Dan would be coming from that direction to return Helen and Becky. I made a quick decision and wheeled the four horses to the left. I felt uneasy about my decision. Just past the town of Yarnell, the road went off the edge of the world. I had traveled the three thousand-foot drop many times in a car. But six miles of steep downhill with a horse drawn wagon would be challenging if not totally insane. Pushing the thought back in my head, I decided to cross that proverbial bridge when we came to it.

We camped that night just a mile short of the Highway 89 connection. Dan dropped the girls off and brought a small bag of groceries. The store he had stopped at was still a day and a half away from us. My depression had faded away and once again I focused on the needs of the horses and my daughters. That evening I noticed a swelling on old Dolly's face. From the location I suspected it was an infected tooth. There were no vets here and we had no money to pay for one if one were available. I patted Dolly sympathetically knowing there was nothing I could do. I tied her out in the deepest grass that night. That was the best I could do for her. We didn't even have any painkillers. Dolly dropped her head and began grazing like she always did. If it was hurting her, she didn't show it.

It was the end of January. The hills around us were spotted with the dull evergreen of oak brush contrasting with the pale dried yellow grass from the summer past. The valley we were entering was flat, surrounded by rolling hills to the west and rocky granite mountains to the east. Giant cottonwood trees spotted the landscape. This was beautiful place, not revealing the desert floor that began a few miles to the south beyond the small town of Yarnell near the edge of the world. We camped at the side of the road next to one of the tall cottonwood trees. We carried buckets of water for the horses from a spring fed pond near the base of the trees. The horses were not drinking as much water as they had in the heat of the summer. Nights were cold and frosty. The days warmed enough to be comfortable. By noon I could take off my coat and let my bare arms enjoy the warm Arizona winter sunshine.

Dolly's swelling had opened on the side of her face, and a tiny trickle of puss oozed down her cheek. The opening was small and after a day it closed up by itself and healed, never returning to bother her again. Perhaps it was a foxtail and not a bad tooth as I had suspected. Whatever it was, her body managed to heal itself, and I was relieved.

We left as early as we could the next morning. Yarnell and a grocery store were just a few miles up the road. When we reached the center of the tiny town I stopped the wagon alongside the curb in front of the market. A large red wagon sticks out in a small town. As soon as we stopped, people started to gather. A shop owner purchased an original colored drawing from me. The price was one hundred dollars. We were rich! Other townsfolk purchased buckles and note cards. We left town with plenty of food and cash to spare.

The road that left Yarnell heading south led to a precipice of giant granite boulders. It split into two roads. The newer one on the left was for traffic coming up the mountain. We went to the right and followed the old original road. Its narrow strip of asphalt snaked its way to the right and disappeared around a corner. Like a string of mountain climbers, we were going to shimmy down the rock face of this enormous mountain jutting out of the desert. It would take us two hours to reach the bottom. I set my knee against the brake. The trace chains on the two teams slackened and we took our first few steps downward. Dusty and Dolly led the way. From the top of the mountain I took a moment to gaze off into the distance that seemed to stretch for a hundred miles. What a view! To the west, I could see the tiny community of Congress, a few miles beyond the base of the mountain. To the left, twenty miles distant, the town of Wickenburg spread out across the desert. Further south and east a brown haze of smog marked the largest land locked city in the world, Phoenix.

My attention went back to the teams. The narrow single lane road wiggled in and out of the boulders, many larger than our wagon. Some protruded out over the road and I had to hug the cliff side of the road to keep the boulders from scraping the top right side of the big wagon. There was no room for error here. The road surface swayed steeply to the left and right depending on the direction of the turn. Fourth Person riding the white mare rode behind to warn vehicles of the big red wagon ahead, taking up most of the road. All the vehicles slowed with caution and passed politely, except for one. A large brown delivery van with yellow letters on its side. It squeezed past us at a rate of speed I thought was dangerous for this road on any day. The man in the brown uniform had whooshed past us before I even knew he was there. Perhaps he did not see the white horse and rider with the red flag waving. I was just thankful he was on the outside edge as he passed.

This road had been used by two-way traffic going up and down the mountain for many years. It was not recommended for vehicles over forty feet long–like us. Since the new lower road had been opened, this one had been turned into a single lane for traffic going down. It was barely wide enough for a car or truck to pass. Every few minutes a car slowly drove around us and went on its way. The speed limits were posted at all of the hairpin turns. Twenty miles per hour for this one, twenty-five for the next, and so forth down the mountain. The normal posted speed was a whopping thirty five miles per hour.

Looking out over the edge of the cliff to my left, I saw the gutted carcasses of cars and trucks that wanted to get to the bottom in a hurry. And that they did. The hard way. The cliffs were so steep that these dead vehicles were left to rot in the desert sun. No effort was made to remove the scrap metal that they had become.

My leg was getting weary from the constant pressure on the brake. It was time to put the 'Burrito the Black' emergency brake into service. This was done by banging the butt end of the buggy whip on the side of the wagon a couple of times a few feet in front of the black mule. His reaction would be to stop, brace his feet and pull back on his lead rope that was tied to wagon. Not in a panic mode, but more of a subdued stubborn action. All four feet gripped the pavement, and the wagon nearly came to a stop. The trace chains tightened and I could release the leg brake for a moment. After the blood recirculated down my leg, I pushed against the leg brake again and let the black mule continue walking. This procedure was repeated down the mountain as my leg went numb. Once again, necessity was the mother of invention. It was the only time on the entire trip that Burrito the Black was put into service. Although he did finally wear a packsaddle, we had no panniers for him to carry. He was just along for the ride.

Half way down the mountain the scenery changed from large granite boulders to smaller rocks. Prickly pear cactus grew out of crevices between the rocks. Isolated patches of dried yellow grass popped up out along the cliff face. We saw the first of the saguaro cacti clinging to the side of the mountain. First one, then as we proceeded further down, another, then many. This was the land of coyotes and road-runners. A habitat for mountain lions and vultures. We were nearing the floor of the Sonoran Desert. The air had gotten warmer. We went around one last curve and the road began to straighten for a short distance. Then one more curve and it straightened, and went down the final slope to the desert floor. We had come down a road that I knew we would never go up. It would not be physically possible. I doubt it had ever been traveled by horse drawn wagon even in the days of the pioneers. It had been a trail for pack mules, widened at the advent of the automobile. The Buffalo Chips and Company wagon had rolled down the old trail. That had been an adventure all to itself.

The road slowly turned towards the south and we followed it into the community of Congress. We crossed the Pea Vine railroad tracks and followed a dirt road led that led off to the left. What was there drew me like a bee to nectar. I could see it from my elevated perch on the wagon. Between the road and the railroad tracks a grove of mesquite trees flourished. Beneath them the green grass grew tall and lush. There was enough to last all our animals needs for nearly a week. Our first day in the desert and we had found an oasis! Each of the horses and mules were staked out to their own mesquite tree. The next discovery would need to be water. With the small water tank wagon we could drive to any place in the community to get water. But that wasn't going to be necessary. A few hundred feet from where I had parked the wagon in the midst of the mesquite trees, was a community center with an outside water spigot. The double front doors were open.

After entering the building I found some retired folks playing checkers and asked about the water for my horses.

"Sure, take all you need" was the reply. We used up the remaining water in the small wagon, and then hooked up the smaller team to it and drove across the road to fill the tank. We would stay here and let the horses pig out on the plentiful grass along the railroad right of way. The only downside to our campsite was that the Pea Vine railroad was forty feet away from our wagon.

The train came through about three o'clock in the morning, everyday. We would feel the vibration before the engineer blew the horn. The wagon shook and the sound was deafening as the train passed only a few yards away. The horses were so trail broke by now they barely gave it notice and focused on the green grass growing beneath them. It took almost a week for the horses to mow down the tall grass from underneath all the trees. As they cleaned up the grass from around the base of one tree we moved them to a new one. In a few days, it looked more like a park, neatly mowed, than a wall of neglected brush waiting for the dry season, and wildfires.

There was a small store only a short walk away and a little Laundromat. Next to it was a tiny hole-in-the-wall café where we splurged and ate a meal. From their front window I could see out to the north to the mountain we had come down a few days before. The two roads across its face left two parallel scars, angling upwards to the summit. You could see their crooked lines crawling across the rocky mountain from many miles away. It was hard to imagine a horse drawn wagon coming down that slope, but we had just done it.

Finally the feed was nearly gone. It was time to move on. We had no time set to be anywhere, but Wickenburg was having a celebration in a few days, and we wanted to be there. Gold Rush Days was a four day event the whole town was involved in. They had old-fashioned melodramas, gunfights in the streets, a carnival, arts and crafts, a rodeo, and a parade. We harnessed up, filled the water tank to the brim, and headed south following the Pea Vine until we turned east on Highway 93. A few miles down this main artery between Phoenix and Las Vegas we turned off onto Vulture Mine Road and again went south. Then three miles later turned east again and headed into Wickenburg. The town is spread out in all directions and has an old west atmosphere to it. A large graded area opened up on the left and we pulled in to camp for the night. The far side of the parking area sloped down into a ravine, where we could tie out the horses. The grass was not as thick here as it had been in Congress, but it would do. The horses were watered and tied out on their long stake out ropes to various Palo Verde trees in the bottom of the ravine. The only other vegetation around was creosote bushes and saguaro cactus. The grass only flourished under the canopy of the Palo Verde trees. Not much grew in this land of sand, rock and sun.

Figure 13. At the Wickenburg Gold Rush Days Parade.

In the morning a couple that owned the local feed store stopped by and offered their back parking area for us to camp in. We took them up on the offer, harnessed up and moved our camp. After staying there for a couple of nights the grass ran out and we moved on to the far side of town. There was a big wash to the east of our new campsite with plenty of grass in the bottom.

Each day I walked into the center of town, armed with poster paints and brushes, looking for work. The local stores paid me to decorate their windows with paintings of bucking horses, team ropers, and such to celebrate the up-coming rodeo. The whole town had a festive atmosphere. We hooked up the small team to the small wagon and managed to make a few dollars with wagon rides. Every little bit helped.

Saturday was the day of the parade. A Phoenix television crew had discovered us, and they rode with us on the wagon at the tail end of the parade. We made the ten o'clock news. When we drove back in to our campsite, my long time friend Marina Darling and her family greeted us. They had driven all the way from southern California to visit. It was good to see a friendly face. Her children enjoyed exploring the desert around the campsite with Helen and Becky that afternoon. Then we took all the children over to the carnival and let them ride a few of the kiddy rides. Marina and her family spent the night at the closest motel, then said their good-byes in the morning and headed home. We planned on leaving the next morning. The Gold Rush Days were over for another year. There was no reason to stay. The crowds were leaving. And so were we.

Once we left Wickenburg, we would be taking the road towards Lake Pleasant. There would be no water readily available for twenty-five miles. The water tank in the little wagon was topped off. We had replenished our Styrofoam cooler with a block of ice, fresh milk, tortillas, and cheese. A few cans of food were on the shelf. We were good to go.

The head count at this point was ten horses and mules, two dogs, two children and two adults. Organized chaos on the move.

The road that went southeast out of Wickenburg was a divided highway. On the right it followed the Hassayampa River bed. Cottonwood trees were thick along that side of the road. Between the trees I could see the sandy river bottom and an occasional glint of water. On the left the road skirted around cliffs of white, yellow and red rock that came straight up out of the ground. Thirty, forty, fifty feet into the sky. Deep narrow canyons split the face of the rock at irregular intervals. Mexican palm trees grew back in some of their recesses. Sometimes a dirt road led up one of the canyons. But more often, the canyons were just a place for flash floods to use on their way downstream into the Hassayampa River. The big red wagon rolled across the Santo Domingo wash bridge and headed uphill towards Phoenix. A mile past the crest of the hill, we turned left at a place in the road known as Morristown. Perhaps there was a Morris there but the town was missing. The only buildings were a post office and an old dilapidated bar. The last of civilization we would see for days. We followed the narrow black strip of road that went east through the desert towards Lake Pleasant. Ten miles distant a ridge of reddish brown mountains beckoned. Beyond them were Lake Pleasant and the road that led south towards the grandmother's home. We camped alongside the road that evening, as we usually did. The vegetation here was mostly creosote bushes, some Palo Verde trees, and the familiar saguaros. The horses had little grass to eat. This was real desert. Pickings were slim. All ten animals were tied out along the right of way fence. As usual the big draft mares were staked where the grass was the thickest. Or in this case, the least thin. Tomorrow would be better, maybe.

By noon the next day we had reached the distant mountains. The road wound up through a shallow pass then crested and sloped down the other side. From the summit I

Figure 14. A campsite near Lake Pleasant, Arizona.

could see the Agua Fria River below. Or where it should have been. There was no river. Just the dry riverbed of where it used to be. To the left a tall earthen dam stopped the rivers flow. The only water that passed below the bridge was in a concrete irrigation canal.

Many years ago, according to a gentleman we all knew as Uncle Dale, the Agua Fria River has been so thick with cottonwood trees and vegetation you couldn't ride a horse through it. All the rivers in Arizona he had seen were that way. He had arrived in Arizona as a boy in 1905 from Kansas. It was still wild country back then. The rivers coming down out the mountains trickled water along their entire length. Though sometimes during the hot summer months the water went beneath the sand and came back up again a few miles downstream. Giant cottonwood trees flanked the water's edge. The rainy seasons and monsoons brought the flash floods. There were wetlands with egrets and other wildlife. Eagles nested in the tops of the cottonwoods. Then the dams were built. The flow of water stopped, and the giant cottonwoods downstream died. Along with all the other vegetation that lived along the river's edge. Most of the wildlife and birds left.

When the dams finally filled, and the excess had to be released, there was no vegetation to slow the man made flood. It scoured the barren river bottom on its way towards the Colorado River. The dead cottonwoods were toppled and scattered along the path of the rushing water. The devastation was complete. Had they allowed some of the dammed up water to continually trickle down the old riverbed, perhaps the loss of trees and wildlife could have been averted. All that it left of the Aqua Fria River now is a sandy white scar a mile wide, skirting the west of Phoenix.

We passed over the bridge and headed up the slope on the far side. As the road turned south a sandy haired man in a small white truck stopped us. A sign on the truck's side read 'A Day in the West'. The driver was Ron Nix, a television stuntman, actor, and owner of a nearby western movie set. He invited us to stay awhile at his old west town. It was open weekends for the public and he said we could give wagon rides and add some color for the tourists. Because we had no agenda, we made a quick decision to check it out. A dirt road a mile ahead turned off to the west. It passed a tiny airport that offered glider rides then went down a slope and back into the wide sandy bottom of the dry Aqua Fria River. We couldn't cross the deep sandy river with the big red wagon so we unhitched the teams and Ron pulled the wagon across with his pickup. He parked it just outside a small arena they used at the movie set. We had mesquite trees for shade. It was a pretty setting with the rocky desert mountains as a backdrop.

Above the arena on a hill stood what looked like an old west town. Buildings of weathered gray clapboard butted up next to each other on both sides of the dirt main street. There was a Livery, a Doctor's office, a General Store, a Chinese laundry and of course, the Long Branch Saloon. Venders selling their wares to tourists on the weekends used some of the other buildings. There was also a tiny restaurant. Ron had built the entire town by himself. He rented it out to people in the movie and television industry as a backdrop for their films. It was really neat. Helen and Becky had run of the town. They thought we had landed in Knotts Berry Farm.

Figure 15. The Day in the West Movie Set.

There were a variety of people that lived there, besides Ron's family. We introduced ourselves to them as we met. It turned out that one of the more shady looking characters was a cousin of Fourth Person. He certainly looked the part of an old west cattle rustler. Tall, and lanky. His face was narrow and his unshaven cheeks sunk in. A cigarette dangled from the side of his mouth. His felt cowboy hat at one time was black but was now covered in a layer of dust with dark sweat marks around the band. Crooked yellow teeth, one of which was broken, smiled broadly as he recognized his kin. He and Fourth Person caught up with the family happenings. Who was in prison, and who had been paroled. It took awhile. He called himself Milo. He was there practicing to be a stuntman/comedian/actor looking for work. In short, he was chronically unemployed and slept in a small cave just past the fake Indian village on the left. I think Fourth Person was envious of his free lifestyle.

A week after arriving Ron told us about an upcoming 'shoot' for a commercial. They would rent our team and driver for a stagecoach shot, and Helen and Becky and I would be used as extras as needed. We were thrilled! I had never been involved in anything like it. A week later a crew showed up with big trucks and professional actors. The first scene I was in was at the Indian village. There were several teepees set up in a nearby canyon, and all I had to do was wrap up in a buffalo robe and sit on our paint horse Prince. That was my acting debut. The next day we harnessed Dolly and Dusty and backed them up to a fake stagecoach. It was not meant to roll. The wheels were nailed solid. It was just a prop. The trace chains were attached to the doubletrees, and Fourth Person climbed up on the seat. He even had a line to say. 'Whoa.' Dusty and Dolly obediently stood patiently for over an hour while the camera crew took different shots and actors acted. Dusty finally took a single step forward and Fourth Person pulled her back. I overheard one of the crew ask, "What happened?" Another person answered, "They bolted". I had to smile. Hollywood people.

The lead actor in this commercial was the first ever winner of Star Search. A good looking young man that had secured a place in this commercial by his winning first place on the show. I recognized another actor from several old west films and commercials. He had fuzzy gray hair that stuck out from beneath his bowler hat. Helen and Becky laughed because he sat around in his under shorts while waiting for his scene, not wanting to wrinkle his pants. He had his hat, shoes, coat, vest and shirt on. His pants neatly folded on his lap. It was a funny sight. Helen and Becky got their turn in the commercial too. I dressed them in long prairie dresses, along with myself, and we were seen running across the street of the old west town fleeing from a gunfight. They paid us well for our efforts. We got a check for six hundred dollars. Fourth Person immediately bought himself a new rifle.

During the days of filming all our meals were catered. On the last night we all met in the local steakhouse and had our final meal there. When a small steak was delivered to Helen she asked me what it was. I smiled and told her, "Its meat, honey. Eat it"'. The people at our table thought it was funny. I couldn't remember the last time we had eaten steak. The closest thing to sirloin I had seen in years was a dead squirrel. A few days after the film crew left an acquaintance of someone at the movie town offered Fourth Person a job. He needed a hand at his gold mine. It was located about twenty-five miles away near the town of New River. The thought of the regular paycheck made my mouth water. The work would be simple. The owner of the mine just needed an extra person in his excavating operation. But I knew how allergic Fourth Person was to work. It would be easier to push a marshmallow into a piggy bank.

Before he accepted the job he insisted the girls and I go with him. We would stay there with him while he worked that week. There was a camper shell at the mine sitting on the ground that we could live in. Whoopee, I thought. It was hard to imagine something worse than living in the horse drawn wagon but here it was. It had a stove and a bed. And a two years supply of dirt and cobwebs. But I wasn't concerned about the cleanup. It was leaving the livestock behind at the old west town that didn't feel right. But this was typical behavior by Fourth Person. He didn't like to go to a job unless I went along. Even if it meant I had to sit in a car and wait. If I refused he would quit and then say it was my fault. He'd blame me and say I wasn't supportive of him. But I knew it was just another of his weird controlling methods. His insecurities seldom allowed me out of his sight. Either way, I lost.

By the time we returned that weekend, I felt deep down that something was wrong. Milo had offered to watch the stock while we were gone. But he had spent most of the week away from the movie set with his new girlfriend. Upon arrival, my apprehension caused me to begin searching almost frantically for the horses. Their safety and well

Figure 16. Author (far right) and daughter watch stuntmen entertain the crowd at Day in the West movie set.

being weighed heavily upon me. I had not been happily separated from them that whole week. I wanted to see with my eyes that all were safe, uninjured, and content. Most of them I discovered close to the arena, nibbling on the mesquite trees that surrounded it. The mules had walked up the canyon towards the Indian village and were eating the short green grass there. I counted heads as I walked along. Making a mental note of whom I had seen and whom I hadn't. One was missing. The new sorrel mare Becky had named Cinderella. Again I searched all over the property. It didn't make sense. She should have stayed close to the group. I walked deeper into the canyons surrounding the old west town. There were no hoof prints in the soft dirt and sand. No fresh droppings. I stopped and asked the people working at the movie set if anyone had seen her and if so, when. No one knew she was missing. Our horses were not their concern. They were mine and I felt I had failed miserably. It didn't take me long to deduce that Cinderella had been stolen. It's not reasonable for a horse to leave its herd unless they had some outside help. The place we were in was remote.

The closest phone was several miles away at the tiny airport. When I finally caught a ride I was able to use the phone to contact the Arizona Livestock Board to report a missing or possibly stolen horse, her description, last location, and her official Arizona Livestock Hauling Ownership Card number. Arizona had begun to issue the cards many years ago. They thought that perhaps it would curtail the rampant horse thefts in the state. I think all it did was provide state employees with job. The cards actually made it easier for the thieves. For instance, Cinderella's card described her as a sorrel mare with no brands or white markings. It had her weight at four hundred pounds at the time of her weaning when the card was first issued. The description matched about five thousand others mares in the state. A horse thief could use a card like this to prove ownership on any sorrel mare with no white markings he managed to get back into his corral. The horse would usually be taken to a local livestock auction and sold within days. Cash in pocket the thief walks away and the horse is never seen again. The system didn't work.

We had no way for an Arizona Livestock Officer to contact us. It had been my experience they were too busy with other things to concern themselves with a missing horse. Because I had no vehicle, the only way I could search for her was by horseback. I did what I could that way but it had been days since she came up missing and my hopes of finding her close by were gone. Strangely, about a week later a young man from the dude stable a few miles away showed up and asked if we would be willing to sell the Arizona Hauling Card on the missing mare. He'd pay us twenty-five dollars for it. There stood the horse thief. I knew he had her. But where? I had looked over the horses at the stable where he worked. There was no sign of her there. I found out later there was another stable in Scottsdale owned by the same folks. Perhaps Cinderella was transported over there. We never saw her again or the young man after we refused to sell him the card. The value of the little mare was not much. Still, it was a disappointing loss. After that incident I refused to return with Fourth Person to the mine. I would stay with the horses. A few days later, he quit. But not before he stole some tiny gold nuggets from his employer, who had foolishly showed him where he hid them.

We stayed at the Day in the West movie town for two months. It was mid April. The saguaros were blossoming. Great white blooms appeared on the tops of the arms of the cacti. The mesquite trees were blooming also, and the desert air was rich with the scent of the springtime blossoms. Beyond the Indian village shallow caves near the top of the steep canyon walls dripped with honey. From the tops of the caves hung long honeycombs, several feet in length, quite visible from the canyon floor. Swarms of bees flitted in and out. The yellow Palo Verde blossoms were alive with bees. The trees hummed.

One weekend a visitor to the town spied Burrito the Black, and purchased him from us. He wanted a pack mule.

No tears were shed from me as they walked the black mule into the horse trailer. It was just one less mouth to feed. He was still as ornery as ever. But still, I would miss him. He had been part of the long trip from Texas to Arizona. He was the first of the group that made the entire trip to leave the party. A few days later, Taco the mini mule found a new home also. Enchilada, the other mini mule had left the troupe months before. We were now muleless. Before we left to go over the river and through the desert to grandma's house, we acquired another sorrel mare. She became Milo's riding horse. Milo would need a riding horse, because he had decided to come with us on our excellent adventure. Misery loves company I thought. Having an outsider along meant I was less likely to get the brunt of Fourth Person's violent tirades and that worked for me. For Milo, it would be a step down from having a cave to sleep in at night, but I suppose the adventure outweighed the loss.

The day came for us to be on our way. Ron Nix had graciously pulled the big wagon back across the sandy river bottom and parked it along side the dirt road leading to his movie set. We rode and led the remaining horses across the river bottom and began the routine of harnessing. In the bar ditch near the wagon someone had thrown away an orange T-shirt. Reaching down, I gingerly picked it up and examined it. Carefully turning it from the front to the back looking for signs of use in lieu of bathroom tissue. It looked new except for the little road dust that had settled on it. There was some screen-printed advertising for a type of racing gear across the back. I shook the dust from it and confiscated it for my personal use. It had been a long time since I had a new shirt to wear. This one was the right size. After a good hand washing, and drying by the desert sun, I would add it to my wardrobe. I was not a high maintenance woman.

Fourth Person decided to drive that day for the first time since we left his parent's place in Texas. Perhaps he wanted to impress Milo with his teamster abilities. My only concern was his lack of awareness to the task at hand. Have you ever noticed how some people, while driving a car, have the ability to run over the only rock in the road or hit the only pothole? Traveling at high speeds you can give a person a little slack, but Fourth Person could manage to hit rocks and potholes at a blazing four miles per hour. Sometimes he even drove off the steep edge of the road completely having then to over correct to get the rig straightened out. Inside the wagon, objects would rattle and bounce from their positions, and sometimes hit the floor. When the small ice chest fell over, melted ice water, ice cubes, sticks of butter and milk spilled everywhere. Had there been a licensing test for horse drawn rigs, Fourth Person would still have his learners permit.

That morning, I had saddled up the stud horse Prince. What a delight he was to ride! We had only gone a mile or so down the road when Fourth Person began insulting me with derogatory remarks in front of his beloved relative Milo. Being horseback, and knowing where we would be camping that night, I simply rode away from the wagon and reined the painted stud to the south directly into the wild desert. Giggling to myself, I trotted off into the forest of mesquite trees, saguaros and Palo Verde's. Away from Fourth Person and his maliciousness. His angry comments faded behind me. The desert opened up in front of me. With Milo present, I knew my daughters and horses would be fairly safe until I met up with them again that night. I smiled as I thought how Fourth Person couldn't even come after me. Milo couldn't drive the horses. Fourth person was stuck with the wagon! "Freedom!" I yelled. And pushed the stallion into a gallop. It was the happiest I had been on the entire trip. Had it not been for the girls and the horses, I could have easily kept going for a long, long, time.

For the next few hours I rode alone. It was refreshing. Fourth Person seldom allowed me out of his presence. I could enjoy the day. The Sonoran desert in the spring is a wonderful place. It's a time when the dead come back to life. The desert floor was decorated with orange poppies, yellow brittle brush, and purple fillaree. Hedgehog cactus blooms displayed their deep metallic maroon color. Quail families flittered about between the giant saguaros. I watched two baby cottontails scurry into the protective brush beneath a Palo Verde tree as I approached. A ground squirrel squeaked from the top of a tall boulder at the side of the trail, indignant that I had invaded his territory. Then flipped his tail and disappeared down the far side. This was a beautiful place. We followed a rabbit trail across the desert towards a small mountain in the distance. The soft dirt alongside the trail bore tracks of lizards, rabbits, and javalinas.

Coming to the edge of a wash, I let the old stud pick his footing through the round river rocks to the sandy bottom a few feet below. To the right I heard a familiar buzz. Upstream in the dry sandy streambed, was a rattlesnake. He was acting oddly, and because I was a safe distance away, stopped the stallion to get a better look. The snake was at least twenty-five feet from the spotted stud and me. It was not my presence that made him buzz. The snake was holding his body and head nearly straight up, about two feet into the air. Half his length. Then I heard a second buzz. Another snake lifted its head out of the sand and assumed the same position. The snakes moved closer together and repeated the performance. Then wrapped their necks around each other. I had stumbled upon their love nest. Lucky me. Not wanting to invade their privacy, I tapped the stud with my heel and pointed him up the far side of the wash. It was certainly springtime. Even for the rattlesnakes.

A mile or so further I encountered a man-made barrier I could not cross. It was the CAP canal. A waterway bringing water to the Valley of the Sun all the way from the Colorado River over a hundred miles away. I would have to ride east until I found a crossing. As it turned out the only crossing was on 99th Ave, the road the wagon would soon be coming down. Deciding to wait, I dismounted and led the stud over to the minimal shade of a mesquite tree. There were no tracks or evidence that the wagon had beat me to this place. They would show up within the hour. And they did. Fourth Person's rage had abated. Trading the saddled stud for the wagon seat, I took up the lines again and drove the wagon the rest of the way to grandma's house.

At the edge of the dry Agua Fria River, about three miles north of Sun City, sat a tiny ten-foot by forty foot prehistoric house trailer. We had made it to grandmas. This had been her home since grandpa had died several years before. She lived next door to her son and his wife. They had been here for decades. Like rings on a tree, you could tell how long by the layers of dead automobiles and junk spreading further and further out into the desert from their core. If rust had value, these people were wealthy beyond imagination.

Parking the wagon close to the grandmother's trailer, we unhooked the horses and turned them out on the Aqua Fria river bottom for grazing. There were just enough mesquite and Palo Verde trees on the east side of the dry bed to allow for good grass growth underneath. In Arizona, what little grass might grow needed the shelter of a tree to do so. The sun baked everything else even in the winter, quickly. The only water source for the horses was near the wagon. And because of that, the horses never wandered too far. Usually they never left the sight of the wagon.

Grandma lived alone with her cats in the tiny trailer. She was poor but generous. The desert around her home was flat and barren except for a few creosote bushes and one stunted ironwood tree. I tried to imagine what life would be like living here in the summer. It must have been even more difficult for an elderly woman. The temperatures regularly topped out at a hundred ten to a hundred fifteen throughout the hot summer months. A white metal sided trailer, even with an air conditioner would be incredibly uncomfortable. Had I known only a couple years later, that I too would be living in a metal trailer within a few hundred yards of here, I might have thrown myself over the cliff into the dry river bottom. It would have been the more humane thing to do. My destiny would be to tough it out for three years without the luxury of electricity and water like granny had. There were worse experiences than living in a horse drawn wagon, as I would soon find out.

While at grandmas, the opportunity arose to catch a ride back to Texas to pick up Rocky, the horse we had left behind with Tommy Miracle. A person known as the Toe Jam Kid from the old west town movie set had invited us to ride along with him to central Texas. He offered to pull his gooseneck horse trailer if we could help pay for the gas. We had just enough money left over from the commercial paycheck to finance the trip. We would be gone less than a week. The relatives here would tend our horses on this end while we were gone.

I was anxious to get my bay gelding back. I missed him. It had been nearly a year since we left him in Tommy's care. Buttons the Appaloosa would be returned at the same time. Also the small wagon Tommy had loaned us. In no time at all, we were driving down Interstate 10 heading east. All five of us crammed into the front of the Toe Jam Kid's pickup. Buttons rode comfortably by herself in the front part of the stock trailer. She had walked a long way. Almost a thousand miles. She deserved the rest. For a now five-year-old horse, she could do anything. Nothing fazed her as she had experienced nearly everything. She was broke to pull a wagon and ride in any situation. Tommy was pleased to see her when we pulled in his drive. She would be a colorful, safe mount for his grandchildren. After we unloaded his little wagon I joyfully put my familiar bay colored gelding Rocky into the trailer. It was good to have him back. The injury on his leg had left a large scar, but he was sound. He had needed more veterinary work, and Tommy had picked up the bill. All I could do was thank him. Years later I tried to find Tommy to repay him for his kindness and generosity, but he had moved on.

From Tommy's, we drove back to Carlton to visit the family I had worked so hard to escape from. They were still having family problems. Fourth Person's younger brother had been arrested for stealing a tanker load of gasoline. This was quite an achievement. When we had left, his biggest haul had been aluminum ladders and chainsaws from the local hardware store. Randy, their baby brother had been caught stealing cattle. His father's. Twenty-nine of them. All sold at the local auction one or two at a time using his dad's own truck and trailer to haul them away. The wealth he had gained by selling his father's assets had been used to furnish his old pickup truck on blocks with a new leather diamond tuck upholstery job. By hocking his mothers four-carat diamond ring, unbeknownst to her, he hoped to buy an engine. He was caught after the fact in that incident. No charges were filed for either crime. Both younger brothers seemed to be trying to attain the criminal status of their big brother, Fourth Person. He was the most successful of the three caballeros. Their older brother, the Fourth Person, was slippery as a Teflon skillet. The only times he had actually been arrested was for buying alcohol for a minor, and beating up a man so badly he was hospitalized for several days. He was their hero. And I was married to him.

My relationship to Fourth Person brought me no special privileges, special treatment or protection in this family of predators. Everyone was fair game. They had perfected the ability to live off of each other. Use and abuse, and no one seemed to care.

One day, for no apparent reason I came home to find my dog missing. This was unlike her, as she would always greet me when the truck pulled in the drive. I had owned her since she was six months old. She had been my special companion for thirteen years. Her name was Dingo. I made the mistake of leaving her behind that day.

Walking towards the grandparent's house, I spied a spot of blood on a stone. Then a place where fresh dirt had been spread over damp spot. Kicking it with the toe of my boot, a dark gooey brick red color appeared. It was blood. I ran to the porch, calling for my dog. More blood soaked the indoor outdoor carpet by the door. A chill went up my spine and I started to cry. Where was Dingo? Running into the house I found fourteen year old Randy at the kitchen table. He smirked at me. Mom and dad were gone, and he had shot Dingo with a rifle, for no more reason than target practice. The first shot did not kill her and she ran to the door of the house looking for protection, and me. He killed her there. Fourth Person grabbed Randy by the collar and forced him to dig a hole. Then we drove out to the place where Randy had thrown her body in a dry creek bed and brought her back. Holding her blood soaked dead body, I stroked her side and cried on the trip back to the grave. I could not and still cannot comprehend such a heinous act. Randy was never held accountable for this act of cruelty.

Fourth Person's parents were having other troubles than their morally challenged sons. They had run up a fifty thousand dollar feed bill at the local mill and were filing bankruptcy. The family farm they had bought four years earlier was going to auction along with their small herd of malnourished and sickly dairy cows.

Having been raised in the dairy industry in southern California as a little girl, I understood what a dairy was *supposed* to look and operate like. My father had worked as a herdsman for a premier six hundred head award-winning farm in Chino. The farm in Carlton was a poster child for what a dairy shouldn't be. The milk they produced was unfit for human consumption and designated for animals. The cows stood in two feet of manure and slop prior to entering the barn. Their udders covered in excrement were difficult to properly clean before slipping on the suction cups attached to the pulsating machines. Mastitis was rampant, spreading from one cow to another via the machines. Cows dying of blue bag were kept in a dark barn on the property, their rotting udders sloughing off. It was a blessing to these poor beasts to be taken over by the creditors and sold at auction a few months later.

Being back at this place brought back other memories. None were pleasant. The first time we came here was not long after the in-laws purchased the place. Fourth Person, being separated because of their move, was chomping at the bit to see dear old Mom and Dad and the sooner the better. They had sold their property in Arizona and relocated to this small dairy in Texas. In a matter of months we were on the road, driving the entire twelve hundred miles almost non-stop. My two daughters were only one and three years old at the time. And I was eight weeks pregnant with child number three. We all sat and slept in the front seat of the old pick up truck, stopping only for potty breaks and gas.

Our arrival was just after midnight. We had been on the road for over twenty-four hours. There were no beds waiting for our arrival. A place in the living room was pointed out where we could sleep on the floor. I put the baby and her older sister on the sofa, and lay down next to it. I was exhausted. The next day an old overhead camper that had been taken off a pickup was designated our guest quarters. It was sitting on the dirt near the entrance to the dairy barn. The overhead part held a mattress and there was a small table that turned down into a bed for the baby and toddler. Inside, everything was covered in a layer of dust and grime. The ceiling was speckled with the tiny black spots deposited by ten thousand flies. I spent part of the day trying to clean the places we would be using.

After dinner that evening, I started having twinges of pain in my lower abdomen. I thought that perhaps it was from something I had eaten. As the evening progressed so did the pain. Before heading back out to the barn where our suite sat, I used the bathroom. I was spotting blood. Hoping it was nothing to be concerned about I went to bed. By eleven o'clock the pains had gotten so severe my cries awoke fourth person. I told him about the blood. He walked with me back down the drive to his parent's house. His mother was a LPN. He could pass my problem off to her. Back inside their home, I immediately went to the sofa and lay down. By this time I was in tears, as the pain intensified. It felt like my insides were been torn out, strip by strip. I cried out as fourth person and his mom decided my fate in the far corner of the room. "She's going to lose it" I heard his mother say. Then I heard the words 'emergency room' and 'doctor' and 'money.' Another spasm shook me. A stifled cry left my lips. I was fading in and out of consciousness. The two came over and stood at the end of the sofa, looking at me. Then the mom told her son "You can't leave her here. She's waking up the whole house!" And with that, the LPN went back to bed.

Fourth Person picked me up by the arm, and led me back to the camper. Two more hours passed. I was bleeding continually now. Soaking up one pad, then another. Trying to hold back my cries, so as not to disturb the baby and her sister anymore than possible. I was thankful they were sleeping through most of it. Fourth Person was also trying to sleep and very unhappy that I kept disturbing him. Then, with no warning, the pain stopped instantly. "The pain has stopped" I said, amazed at my relief. Almost before I finished the statement, a warm mass of fluid and tissue expelled from my body. I had miscarried. Fourth Person scooped up the mass and placed it in a paper grocery bag. Then he left the camper. When he came back, he told me he had buried it in a corner of the cow pasture. Being in shock, from trauma and blood loss, I said nothing.

It was almost daylight. I had fallen into a fitful sleep. The sun did not come up that morning. Everything was shrouded in a gray fog. Fourth Person steadied me as I stood and guided me back to the parent's house. I leaned against the bathroom wall, as he put a small metal folding chair in the shower, turned on the water and walked away. I sat in the shower, on the cold metal chair, and cried.

I was beginning to panic that I would be abandoned at this place again and was very happy to see a truck arrive. The short family visit ended when Toe Jam returned, pulling in the long gravel drive. The very same drive we had left over a year ago in the wagon. This time Rocky would ride to Arizona. And he would have company in the trailer on the ride back. A neighbor had left two horses and a pony in the family's care then moved away. With a bankruptcy around the corner, we ended up taking them back to Arizona with us. There was a yearling Shetland filly, and an older gray mare that had a yearling Appaloosa colored stud colt with her. The trip back was made non-stop. The horses were happy to get out of the trailer after a twenty four-hour drive and stretch their legs. We all were. It was good to be back in the desert, and far away from the family. At least for a little while. After going belly up, they moved back to Arizona. It would only be a few months until their arrival in the Phoenix area.

The desert had already become much warmer upon our return. The sunshine hinted of extreme heat on its way and we didn't want to be here to greet it. We planned to spend the summer in the high country, and prepared to head north again from whence we had come. This time we would not use the same route that brought us here but head straight north. The only fly in that ointment was Interstate 17. We would have to use it between Black Canyon City and Rock Springs, a distance of about eight miles. Not that it would be a problem for the wagon, but if seen by the highway patrol, they could be a problem for us. But it was a chance we would have to take. There were no access roads through the desert between those two towns. The only other routes were through Payson, a hundred miles out of our way, or back up Yarnell Hill, and that was definitely not an option.

We bid farewell to grandma and the adjacent relatives and rolled out the long dirt road towards 99th Ave to the east. Helen was again riding Peter Pony. Milo was riding the new small sorrel mare, Fourth Person sat atop Rocky, and I drove the wagon. Two miles away from grandmas, the local newspaper caught up with us and took pictures. Once again we made the local news. Camp that evening was alongside a graded gravel road to the east of Lake Pleasant. We were about eight miles away from New River, a tiny desert town north of Phoenix.

The three new horses had done well on their first day on the trail. The yearling Appaloosa gelding was leading nicely. The sores across his nose were closing and healing without any problems. Back at the family farm in Carlton, no one seemed to notice, or care, that the halter he wore perpetually needed to be removed. It apparently had been put on him as a foal, and now his head had grown over and around it. It had to be cut off. How he managed to eat was questionable. The halter was so tight I couldn't see how he could open his jaws. The nylon strap across his nose had disappeared beneath the hair and skin causing a deep indentation. Fearing the worst, I cut one side of the strap and slowly pulled it sideways and out of the trench it had created. The poor horse hardly reacted, and calmly stood while I removed the nylon, inch by inch. The skin was hairless in the bottom of the now open wound. It was raw, but not bleeding. After adjusting his new larger halter to fit so that it would not rub against the sore area, I applied a Furazone ointment. Remarkably, his skin and hair returned to normal, leaving only a hint of a scar across his nose.

That evening at the first nights camp there was very little feed for the horses. The terrain was mostly malapai rocks, cholla cactus and dirt. A few sprigs of dried yellow grass appeared at the base of the cacti, where the horses carefully removed them. That night there was no moon. The black desert sky was crisscrossed with millions of brilliant white points of light. The arms of the Milky Way stretched across the sky. The air was cool but not cold. The wail of a coyote came in the distance, answered by the braying of wild donkeys from a canyon near the lake. Night birds warbled on the soft breeze. The Sonoran desert at night is enchanting.

After giving all the horses a good drink that morning, the storage tank, now parked back inside the big red wagon, was nearly dry. Tommy's extra small wagon was missed but we would make do. It was harder to fill the tank inside the wagon, but doable. A hose could be stretched through the doorway. Losing the more compact vehicle would thwart our ability to make side trips that were not easily accomplished with the bigger wagon. But with less mobility came less weight for the horses to pull.

By mid day we found a place close to the Agua Fria River to camp. The creek flowed haphazardly at this point, above the lake and the dam. Large cottonwood trees survived along the creek edge. Vegetation was thick along the boulder strewn river bottom. Pools of water only a few yards wide appeared and disappeared under the rock and sand along its length. Following a dirt road in towards the river we parked close to one of the cottonwood trees. Grass was available in patches up and down the riverbank and we tied the horses out accordingly. Some even had pools of water within their reach.

The next day would be stressful. We would have to travel for two hours along the side of the interstate to reach Black Canyon City. The decision was also made to introduce the new gray mare to the harness, and have her join the team. She was somewhat tired from her two-day trip, and it was a good time to start her. She would be replacing Buttons. All the saddle horses that had been on the trip eventually ended up in harness. Except Rocky. He was too valuable as a saddle horse. But the others could be rotated as needed, giving everyone a rest from the daily grind.

The next morning I walked over to the new gray mare and said to her "Blue, this is a collar". Then I secured it around her neck. Next came the jingling harness, which she paid no attention to. It wasn't much different from the saddle she was already used to. When Dusty and Dolly were hooked to the front of the tongue and Prince the stud secured behind in his position, I walked the gray mare over and fastened her next to the stud, behind Dolly. All four horses stood patiently while I climbed up to the wagon seat. The seasoned horses would stand quietly until I picked up the lines. Then they *knew*. The command to move out would be next.

As I called out the familiar "Dusty, Dolly, giddup!" the big red mares moved forward. The stud moved out in unison, and the gray mare, a bit perplexed, hesitated for a moment, then decided she would go, too. It only took her a few steps to get into sync. The horses surrounding her gave her a sense of security, and calmed her uncertainties. Until her first real challenge, the cattle guard a half-mile up the road. The two four by eight sheets of plywood were taken down from off the wagon roof and placed across the iron bars of the cattle guard, separating us from the highway. All four horses stood patiently, three of which already knew the routine. But this would be a new experience for Blue. She would have to walk across a piece of plywood.

When all was ready I clucked again and tapped the lines across the rumps of the closest team. Dusty and Dolly methodically moved forward and calmly walked over the wood sheeting. When it became apparent to Blue that she was next, with no where else to go, she decided to go straight up, and tried to jump the whole thing. Unfortunately, she was tethered to the wagon tongue and didn't get quite as airborne as she had hoped. Her inside leg came down on the outside of the trace chain. Which made the next few steps difficult. By the time she had come down, all four horses were safely across the cattle guard. The teams were stopped, and the trace chain unhooked and re-attached properly on the outside of her hind leg. Blue had scratched the inside of her leg a tiny bit, just enough to knock off some hair. The four by eight sheets of plywood were thrown back onto the wagons flat roof while the two teams of horses stood. Walking calmly again, the cattle guard now behind us, all four horses continued pulling the wagon up the ramp onto the two-lane Interstate heading north.

It was mid morning, and the traffic heading north from Phoenix was light. The next and only exit was eight miles up the road at Rock Springs. We were walking along the paved shoulder. The spring desert was quite colorful along the highway edge but my focus was on making the next exit before we were spied by the highway patrol. I clucked to the horses and pushed them into a trot hoping to cut our traveling time in half. It would still take an hour. Milo and Fourth Person were riding their horses between the road and the highway fence.

We had managed to cover about half the distance when the flashing lights of a highway department cruiser pulled in behind us. We're toast, I thought. The two outriders rode back towards the wagon as the Highway Patrolman walked alongside the wagon to where I was sitting, holding the lines to the four horses stopped in front of me. He was mad. "You have to turn this vehicle around immediately and get off this highway now!" he yelled. "Sir," I replied, "This vehicle is too long to make the sharp turn back into on-coming traffic. If I swing these horses around, we will block both lanes. Then be facing the wrong way. Please sir, we just need to get to the next exit, a mile or so up the road. "He was perplexed. Our unique scenario posed a multitude of problems for the officer to deal with. I could see the wheels in his head start to turn. If he arrested us, he would have to find a way to deal with all the horses. That could take hours. It would take several horse trailers to remove them all at once. Or several trips if only one could be found. And where would he find someone to drive the wagon? I toyed with the thought of telling the officer "Here, you drive them!" but common sense saved the day and I kept my mouth shut.

Milo and Fourth Person had joined the group. The officer's attention turned toward both riders. He questioned Milo, and asked to see his Id, which he did not have. I chuckled to myself as Milo gave him his fake name, Milo Macintosh. I'm sure had he used his actual name, he would have been picked up on an outstanding warrant. Fourth Person had no Id either, but gave his actual name.

I'm sure it finally occurred to the officer, that arrests would be a bad move, as he would then have no one experienced to move the wagon off the highway. Teamsters experienced enough to drive a four up hitch of horses were few and far between. Especially in the middle of the desert. Having several trailers show up to contain all the livestock would be next to impossible. It was best to just let us roll. After vehemently stressing to us that we would indeed get off the highway at the next exit, he drove away. Good call! It was a win win for both parties. The problem would take care of itself. And we would arrive where we intended too. I didn't waste any time getting the wagon moving again.

I could see the exit for twenty minutes before we arrived at it. It was a big relief for me to turn the horses towards the off ramp and drive to the top of it. Once again, at the cattle guard, the sheets of plywood came down from the top of the wagon, to allow the horses to walk across. Blue did much better this time. Instead of trying to jump it, this time she chose to try to run across it at quickly as possible.

Swinging to the left at the stop sign, we crossed the highway below on the overpass. Then turned right at the frontage road, and drove into the small burg of Black Canyon City. I stopped the wagon in front of the only grocery in town, and we stocked up on the few staples we could afford to buy. While waiting, a local came up to the wagon and told us of a nice campsite, right on the Agua Fria river to the west of town. He said there was plenty of room to turn the wagon around when we got there. I liked the idea. We would be out of sight of any officers of the law and the horses would have plenty of water. Hopefully, there would be some grazing available.

We took the gentleman's advice and followed the road through the neighborhood behind the market to the river. It was everything he said it would be. We parked the wagon within a few yards of the river on a wide flat spot. The river was only a few inches deep on this side. On the other side, less than twenty-five feet away, the water sometimes pooled in depths of one or two feet. Cottonwood trees, along with Arizona Ash grew thick along the far bank. And grass! Deep, thick, green grass, some nearly three feet tall grew out of the gravel and sandbars along the rivers edge. It was horse heaven. And we had plenty of time to let them graze till their bellies were full. During the week that we camped there only one other person came down to our campsite. No one bothered us or cared that we were there.

Helen and Becky played everyday in the shallow water, making tiny boats of leaves and sticks to watch them float away. We took day hikes exploring the desert up and down the rivers edge. For being so close to a small town we were very isolated. The horses had the best time of all. It was early June and the desert sun was starting to get brutal. They spent the days grazing freely along the riverbank in the shade of the cool cottonwood trees. All were released

from their tethers after the first day, and allowed the freedom to move together as a herd while they grazed, rolled,
slept and splashed in the water. With an abundance of feed
and water they never left sight of the wagon.

It was delightful to see the big mares standing belly
deep in the water, eating the green grass alongside the
bank. It reminded me of photos I had seen of moose grazing in Canada. By the time we moved on, all had packed on
a few extra pounds. I didn't want to leave. I'm sure the
horses had they a vote, would have agreed with me.

The dirt trail leading to the higher country was the
original stage route between Prescott and Phoenix. It followed the basin at the bottom of the Bradshaw mountains
eastern edge. In places it was rocky, steep and narrow. Arrangements were made to have the big red wagon towed to
a spot at the top of the hill, where the horses coming up the
stage route would rendezvous. It would be a two thousand-
foot climb over fifteen miles for the horses. Milo and
Fourth Person rode and herded the others up the trail. One
rider in front was leading the alpha mare and the other rider
rode behind to keep the stragglers moving. The girls and I
rode along with the wagon. It was pulled by a pick-up
along Interstate 17 to the Wild Horse Basin exit then west
to the stage route. The place we were dropped off with the
wagon is known as Cordes. It's just a point where two dirt
roads crossed in the middle of nowhere. We arrived there
before noon. It would be several hours before the horses
showed up. After making lunch for the girls, we set out
buckets of water for their arrival. After their long hike I
knew they'd all be thirsty. It was almost sunset when I
heard the pounding of hooves to the south. Then over the
downward slope of the road I saw the head of one of our
horses, then another. Within minutes, all the horses had arrived at the wagon and eagerly drained the tubs of the water. They were tired, and thirsty. It had been a long haul. As
they drained the buckets I refilled them, until one by one,

the horses walked away to graze on the closest available grass.

By evening the next day we were camped on a hilltop overlooking the town of Mayer. Another days walk would lead us back to Prescott Valley. As we left the town of Dewey, the hooves on the yearling Shetland began to bleed. At that point Milo and Fourth Person lifted her onto the porch of the wagon where she could ride. The eighty-mile walk from grandmas had worn her hooves down to the quick. Unlike the larger horses, she had no shoes. I took some rags and wound them around her front feet to ease the pain, and she rode in style until her feet grew out. The girls enjoyed having her living with them. At night she would be staked out in the softest dirt I could find. It would be a month before her hooves grew out again. Amazingly she did not get abscessed.

We spent one night in Prescott Valley, near my parents, and then drove on into Prescott on Willow Creek Road. On the outskirts of town there was an old abandoned arena owned by the city. Next to it was a large fenced pasture. It would be a good place to camp. The arena had a water tank inside, but no water in it. I looked around for a spigot and found one hiding in the tall dry grass. I had doubts as to if it was still working. It had been years since this arena had been used. But a quick turn of the handle proved my suspicions to be false. After a moment of rust colored water passing, fresh, clean water spurted from the faucet.

The arena had overgrown with weeds and grass. After checking to see that all gates were secure, we turned all the horses but the draft mares into it. Dusty and Dolly we led to the adjacent fenced pasture and led through the gate. This five-acre pasture separated the arena from an electrical substation. I had no idea who it owned it. It may have belonged to the power company, or the city, or a private owner. What I did know, was that it had never had any livestock in it in all the years I had lived in the area. The grass was deep and

I didn't think anyone would mind if the red mares ate down the fire hazard. We were there for a month, and no one said a thing.

Milo took up residence in the old announcer's stand at the edge of the arena. It was a three-sided shed on stilts overlooking the arena. It was our plan to be in Prescott for the Fourth of July, the biggest event of the year. Prescott claimed to have the World's Oldest Rodeo and people came from all over for the event. There was a big parade, an art show on the town square and other activities all week long. With Prince saddled I rode the three miles into town with my paints in the saddlebags, hoping to find some windows to decorate for the upcoming rodeo. We were broke, again. I needed to come back to the wagon with food. As it turned out, several of the shops on the town square paid me to paint western themes on their windows. I rode the old stud back to the wagon with saddlebags full of refried beans, tortillas and cheese.

The next day I rode back into town and painted more windows. That weekend was the Fourth of July. We did not have money to go to the rodeo. So we spent the Fourth at the wagon just like any other day. It was enough to be out of the desert heat and to be able to let the horses take a break. I had no idea where we would go from here. Milo grew bored and hitched a ride back to Phoenix. We had no goals. Fourth Person thought living like we were was the epitome of life. I however, was yearning for a home, where I could plant a garden, and put down roots in more ways than one. The thought of living in the wagon forever sent chills up my spine. I did not want to be a professional gypsy. A regular paycheck would have been nice and owning a refrigerator instead of a Styrofoam box. Simple things like electricity and a stove that didn't stink when you used it. A toilet that flushed. A hot shower. The problem with my thoughts of luxury was that I had a husband that would not work. He was happy being a derelict. My future and the future of my girls looked dim.

Around the end of July, we decided to hit the road again for a short trip over to Coyote Springs, a remote area north of Prescott Valley. There was a person there that we knew and the open prairie there had plenty of grass. Though we didn't know it at the time, it would be the last time we drove the wagon along highway. The trip took less than a day. We camped about five miles north of Highway 89A just to the west of Coyote Springs Road. The place was desolate. There was a dirt cattle water tank a few hundred yards away. We spent a week there, walking the horses twice a day to water then staking them out on the rolling prairie. A person living further out came by one day and bought the little Shetland filly. Her feet had grown out and she was back to normal. He had a five-acre pasture for her to live on.

Another resident offered us his fenced ten-acre parcel for a stipend. It was only a mile away, so we harnessed up the mares once more, and drove the wagon over to it. It would be good to let the horses off their tie out ropes, as they could have the ten acres to roam free on.

An old time friend of ours, Ann Heckethorn, who lived not far away, offered us the use of her old car while we were there. What a luxury to have a car! Unlike the horses, it would not be able to graze on the local vegetation. Money was needed to fill the gas tank. With great apprehension, I suggested Fourth Person try to find work. There was a window factory in Prescott Valley that had a reputation of hiring just about anybody. I did not hold my breath but Fourth Person said he'd see about it. A few days later, he was working the night shift. I couldn't believe it. He had a *job!*

Pushing back the thought of how long this one would last, I went about my daily chores. Home schooling the girls and tending the livestock. Because there was no water on the property, I still had to walk the horses down to the cattle tank to drink twice a day. One morning, while Fourth Person slept, I saddled up my gelding Rocky and went for a ride. It was a beautiful summer day. I rode east towards a low range of oak brush covered hills. Coyote Springs was like a development gone bust. Long ago roads had been graded running like lattice across the rolling prairie. Trees here were non existent. Houses were few and far between, sometimes miles apart. The electricity stopped at the highway five miles away. Those that lived out here survived with generators, solar panels, and propane refrigerators. Except for the graded roads every mile or so the land was open and wild as it had been for thousands of years. The few fences that existed were around the handful of residences to keep the open range cattle out. Gamma grass and chino grass grew tall for miles in all directions. Antelope in small herds called this valley home. The morning sun warmed me as I rode east along a rabbit trail. On a hill across from me I could see the scattered bleached white bones of a long dead cow.

Coming finally to a fence a several miles east of the wagon I turned north and followed it. On a hill to my left I heard the sound of tinkling bells. Rocky turned his head to focus on the noise as it grew closer. Then like giant popcorn, a herd of angora goats came bounding over the hill towards us. Rocky panicked. He wasn't sure what those things were but he didn't want to get a closer look. I kept him from bolting to the left or right. Rocky had no alternative other than to back up, which he did at great speed until I was able to calm him. A woman came over the hill, chasing after her goats, which now had us surrounded. Rocky decided his life was not threatened and these were not the demons he thought they were. The woman apologized for her goat's bad manners. Her name was Debbie Hodges. She lived in a tiny house just over the hill. We introduced ourselves and became instant friends. I told her about the wagon trip we had been on and how I yearned to settle down to a normal life somewhere. Then headed back to the wagon. Fourth Person would be awake soon, and I had better be close by.

Figure 17. The sign at the original Turtle Rock Ranch.

The road I followed back towards the wagon had an empty house on it. It looked as though someone had started the project and walked away from it before it was finished. The property was fenced but had the look of abandonment. There was no landscaping, no driveway, just an unpainted slump block house standing bleak in the middle of nowhere. A weathered sign was attached to two small galvanized posts near the gate. On it were the words Turtle Rock Ranch. The closest residence was the goat farm, a mile behind me. It stood isolated, just a small dot on the vast prairie.

A few days later, I rode back over to visit with Debbie. I asked her about the empty house and she gave me the phone number of the owner. Their names were Jim and Dana Nichols. He was an attorney that lived out of state. I had little hope of being able to move into a real home but it wouldn't hurt to ask. I tried to think of what I would say to this big city attorney. "Hi, my name is Marilyn. I just drove a team and wagon all the way from Texas, which I'm still living in, and would like to know if you'd rent that empty house out to me. We're broke, but my husband has had a job for a whole week now. I make a few dollars selling my western art. I have two daughters, and ten horses." It sounded incredulous, even to me.

When I arrived back at the wagon, the family jumped into the car and I took them back over to the house. Fourth Person didn't like the idea. It smelled like commitment and responsibility. Although neither of us had much expectation that we would be allowed to live there, we drove into town and the phone call was made. Much to my surprise Mr. Nichols seemed intrigued by our wagon travel and was interested in my western art. He thought having someone there at the house was a good idea and then said he'd send us a check to cover some repair and maintenance. I was stunned. We had a house to live in! Not a wagon, or a barn, or a tent, or a camper, or a garage, but a house! A real house! The fact that it had no electricity was of no concern to me. Or that the only water was gravity flow from the storage tank. We had been given the keys to a three bedroom, two bath house. I felt rescued. Mr. Nichols set our rent at one hundred eighty dollars a month. That seemed easy enough to handle with Fourth Persons new job. And it would have been, had he not quit three weeks later. Right about the time I discovered I was pregnant.

Dusty and Dolly were hooked up to the wagon by themselves and pulled it the two miles to our new house. I swung the mares through the gate and around the back then unhooked them. It would be the last time that I did so. Our traveling days were over. Buffalo Chips and Company had come to the end of the trail. We had been living in the big red wagon for a year and a half. At the time, I wasn't sure our adventure on the road had really come to an end. We still had the wagon, the harness and the teams. But we had no place to go. Fourth Persons parents had moved from Texas to Arizona, and once again he was drawn to move back in with them. That way he wouldn't have to worry about silly things like rent, and food. Or a home for a new baby.

My pregnancy caused me stress beyond measure. It would be a home birth, like the one before. I was never allowed to see a doctor. I would not have a midwife. Those were things that cost money, which we didn't have, nor would Fourth Person permit me to obtain. I was on my own.

In late September, Fourth Person went into a rage about a visit I had with my parents without his permission. He lit in to me like a wild gorilla. The more I cried out the more I was beaten. After his anger abated, he told me how sorry he was and promised to never do that again. No, I thought, you'll probably use a gun. Debbie stopped by later the next day and when Fourth Person went outside I lifted my shirt and showed her the huge black marks on my breasts, ribs and back. She implored me to leave. I told her to say nothing. I couldn't leave. He had threatened to kill the girls if I did. I was trapped. I could only continue to hope things would get better. But they didn't. It just got worse.

The elevation where we now lived was almost mile high. The winters, even though we were in Arizona could get very cold. In early November I woke to find Dolly lying down. All the other horses were up and grazing on the tall dried grass. I got dressed and walked out to where she was. The frozen ground crunched beneath my boots. Dolly lifted her head and nickered at me as I approached. Something was wrong. I could tell from scrapes on the ground that she had been trying to get up. I went back to the wagon and got a halter and lead and Fourth Person and we tried to get her up. The most she could do was stretch her front legs. There was no effort to stand. I brought her out some water in a bucket and a scoop of grain, which she eagerly ate. A fierce cold wind had begun to blow. I wanted to get her back to the house near a shelter, but she wouldn't budge. The temperature was dropping and pellets of ice began to hit. With a feeling of helplessness I brought out two blankets and covered the old mare as best I could. The icy wind blew unimpeded across the prairie. I checked on her frequently throughout the day, angry that there was no money or even a phone to call a vet. Each time I went out I recovered her with the blankets that had blown off in the wind. I sat with her. Talking, encouraging. Then night came, and I had to go care for my family.

Early the next morning, I jumped out of bed and looked out the window, hoping to see the mare missing from the spot she had lain in. But she was still there. A red boulder shaped object contrasting with the bleak yellow prairie around her. The blankets had blown off again. I dressed quickly and went out to check on her. This time, she did not lift her head at my approach. She lay still, her great rib cage no longer expanding and contracting with her breath. The great old mare had died.

With Dolly's death I knew there would be no more wagon travel. We had no money to purchase another draft horse. And Fourth Person really didn't want to go back to anything but his parent's house, now in Phoenix. In December he announced he was going back to college. I thought this was amusing, because he had never finished high school. The junior college he would attend was only a few miles away from his parents. So it only made sense to move there. My heart sank. I had just walked twelve hundred miles to escape these people and now I was going to once again be living with them. Because a younger brother and his wife already had the spare bedroom we could have a place in the garage.

Nobody likes to read a story without a happy ending. And this story will finally have one, but I must jump ahead a few years before it happens. The red wagon did roll again. But it was not us that drove it. After Dolly died, we stored the Buffalo Chips and Company wagon back at grandmas. A couple that we had met in Dublin Texas somehow managed to track us down, and bought the wagon from us along with Dusty, and Blue. Then they bought another draft mare to be Dusty's teammate. Because they wanted a lighter load, for some reason beyond my common sense thinking, they cut the big red wagon in half, by taking the top four feet off. Now they had no roof. Their plan was to go to Montana. I don't know if they ever reached their destination. Years later I heard that they did make Utah, and that they were now divorced and the wife moved to Florida.

Our old paint stallion was put down due to cancer less than a year after Dolly died. Rocky, my gelding lived with me until he died just a few years ago, at the ripe old age of thirty-five. Peter Pony also lived well into his thirties and I kept him until he also died. My son was born, at home, at the Turtle Rock Ranch house in the spring of 1985. Although we had once again moved in with Fourth Persons parents, I traded my artwork to Mr. Nichols in lieu of rent, so that I would not deliver my son in his grandparent's garage. A few days before I was due, we drove back up to the Turtle Rock Ranch house, and before the weekend was out, I delivered a healthy baby boy. In a house with no electricity. By Coleman lantern. Alone.

Fourth Person did indeed go back to college. He went back, again and again. To collect student grants and student loans. But not to attend school. He managed to do this for seven semesters. Sign up, collect the money, and quit school a few weeks later. I have no idea why they allowed him to do this over and over again. And because there was money for nothing, he encouraged me to go also. Which I did, eagerly. I signed up for art classes. All of them. It was an excuse to get away from his family, and something I enjoyed. I even took a pottery class and learned how to throw my own pots. Because of my previous experience painting gourd ornaments and such, I transferred my designs to the pottery that I had made. And then a funny thing happened.

One evening when I went into class, my locker had sticky notes all over it. The pottery that I had made and painted had been fired and had come out of the kiln. People wanted to buy it! I sold every piece that I had made. The next week I made some more. And I sold that too. A person in the class with me suggested I make up a good selection and take it to her church bazaar. The cost for a space would be only five dollars. Because I didn't even own a table to display my pottery on, I used two fifty-five gallon drums with a four by eight piece of plywood for the tabletop. I covered it with a sheet off my bed. By the end of the day, I had sold sixty-five dollars worth of my pottery. It had been a long time since I had seen so much money.

After my son was a few months old, I took a job as a cashier at a chain drug store. My hours of work were from eleven at night until eight in the morning. I also attended college full time. My first class was at ten or eleven, depending on the day of the week, so I managed to get a little sleep after work. Fourth Person was okay with this. He would stay home all day, play Pac man on his new Commodore 64 and occasionally look after the children. Helen and Becky had been enrolled in school, but more than once I came home to find bruises on the baby. I recognized them and knew how they got there.

Because of my job I was able to get a loan for a house trailer. A cheap metal-sided singlewide that we parked near grandmas on a two-acre piece of desert the parents had invested in. It was pathetic with no electric or water supply, but it was better than the garage and moved us out of the parent's house. My small paycheck would cover the one hundred twenty-seven dollar a month payment. There was an electrical pole within six feet of the trailer with power, but it would not be hooked up unless a septic system was put in. And the family chose not to spend money on property improvements.

We lived for three years in the desert with no electricity or air conditioner, in a metal box. Water was obtained by putting six fifty-five gallon drums in the back of a pickup and driving fourteen miles to the family's house. Then slowly filling the six barrels with a garden hose. Fourth Person liked to do this. He would leave about the time the sun started getting hot and spend the day in the air conditioned comfort of the family's house, eating their food, watching television and drinking coffee with his dad.

Because the septic was never put in, the contents of the toilet dropped to the ground beneath the trailer. Fourth Person eventually dug a hole at the end of the trailer and piped the sewage into it. The toilet was flushed by bringing a five-gallon bucket in from the water trough and pouring it into the bowl. This was done daily. But not by Fourth Person. One day I decided to turn the task over to him. I let him know, without making him angry that the chore would be his. The only other time I have ever seen a toilet overflowing with waste was in Tijuana. Finally, after two weeks the rim had been reached and not a single bucket had been brought in to wash it down. Finally in disgust, I walked out to the water trough and carried the bucket in and took care of it. What depths of laziness did a person have to reach to not be able to flush a toilet? It was beyond my comprehension.

Figure 18. A sample of the authors hand made pottery.

During the three years of my refinement by fire in the desert, my pottery making blossomed. The job at the store had come to an end and I threw myself into my art. The hard work and long hours paid off. I was happy to be working at home, where I could keep my children safe. On weekends I would take them with me to arts and crafts shows where I sold my pottery. It was a small but steady income. Eventually a small studio became available for me just a few miles away. I filled it with pottery, and sales to the locals were good. From out of the blue, Fourth Person got a job. He was hired to lead a camel at an old west amusement park. The camel's name was Daisy. My husband was a camel jockey but it was a job and I was delighted. I had been making the payments on the metal-sided trailer for two years now. With his new job, I hoped he could help out. "Just make one payment," I pleaded. Then waited. The payment due date came, then past. Then went past thirty days and the phone calls started. Just before the second payment due date passed, Fourth Person came home with a brand new pair of two hundred dollar bat wing chaps.

When the mortgage company called again I handed the phone to bat man. After hanging up, he said we should move back in with his parents. I agreed with him. *He* should move back in with his parents. Several more weeks passed. His threats and tantrums continued. Once he grabbed a rifle and went to his knees, putting the barrel in his mouth. He threatened to kill himself if I didn't submit to his demands. When I saw the gun I ran. He was too cowardly to kill himself but crazy enough to shoot me. I grabbed the baby on my way out the door. The time had come for us to part ways. He moved back in with his parents. It had been a long time coming.

Freedom! I had stashed enough money back from my pottery sales to immediately catch up on the payments. It was hidden in my tampon box. I was confident no man would contaminate himself by touching such a thing as a tampon box. Anything hidden inside was secure. A man would sooner pick up a live rattlesnake.

With the trailer payments current, I focused on my bright future. To establish credit, I bought Helen and Becky a full size canopy bed with a matching dresser and a desk for doing homework. The salesman offered insurance for the items for another five dollars until they were paid in full. It was a good thing I took him up on the offer. Three days after the furniture was delivered the trailer burned to the ground with all its contents. The trailer was flattened. Everything was destroyed by the fire. Interestingly enough this occurred after Fourth Person had removed all of *his* things. Including most of the furniture. All of the usual things were lost. Many of my oil paintings, family photos, clothing, etc. Things irreplaceable. I had just begun divorce proceedings, and now this. I was homeless. A friend I met at an art show offered me her extra bedroom that day until I could get on my feet again. The very next morning a gentleman from my pottery class at the college pulled up in front of her house with a carload of pottery for me to paint.

Within hours of losing everything I was back to work. That next weekend I sold enough to pay my divorce attorney's retainer. People from the community who knew me gave me a mattress set, towels, and several boxes of household items. I rented a tiny storage unit to house them. The Red Cross bought the children some clothing. Eight weeks after the fire, I found Jim Nichols phone number and called to inquire about the Turtle Rock Ranch. Was it available? Remarkably, it was. The previous renters had just moved out. He told me where to get the key, and said he'd send a check to cover some improvements. I cried.

On Thanksgiving weekend, Helen, Becky, my three-year-old son, and I moved back into the house where my son was born. I was home. It was time to go to work. For me that meant providing a stable home for my children and earning enough money to provide for all their needs. I could not count on any child support from Fourth Person. Married or not. He would rather go to jail than pay the monthly fifty dollars designated by the courts for all three children. And to jail he went, but it changed nothing.

Just after Christmas that year Helen walked into the kitchen and found me seated at the kitchen table, crying. "Why are you crying mama"? She asked. I looked at her and told her they were happy tears. I had just paid off all the bills, and we had money left over.

In the pasture behind the house, Rocky neighed impatiently for his breakfast. Life was good. I had learned to appreciate the simplest of things. Electricity, running water, and a toilet that flushed. I was so grateful for a roof over my head and a safe place to raise my children. Welfare was never an option for me. I had the capability to earn enough income through the sale of my pottery to make ends meet. I was content with what I had. For the next four years I lived alone with my children. Attending art shows nearly every weekend around the southwest. Traveling in a pick up truck instead of a wagon.

For the next twenty years, I produced pottery to provide for my family. I met and later married a Phoenix business-man named Bryon Wiley. His business background prompted a change in the pottery sales from retail to whole-sale. We called the line of pottery we produced the Turtle Rock Ranch Collection. Bryon did all the casting. Some-times as many as eighty molds a day. My older sister Elaine who had recently moved into the area prepped the pottery for painting, and I painted. We had a lot of orders to fill. Our accounts were nationwide. Over eighty stores sold our hand-painted stoneware pottery. At peak production we employed eight people. In 1999, we moved the Turtle Rock Ranch to Bagdad, Arizona.

In Bagdad, we were fortunate to lease a ranch owned at the time by the Phelps Dodge mine. Not only did it have a beautiful home; it also had a roping arena, corrals, several barns and steel buildings that we used for the pottery manu-facturing. Along with this, there were miles of fenced pas-ture. During our ten years there, I purchased another Paint stallion named WWR Boot Scootin' and began a small breeding operation. Eventually we had ten well-bred mares and sold their offspring as far away as England.

Just before Christmas in 2004, my gelding Rocky died and we buried him there at the ranch. That was a very sad and painful day for me. I had owned Rocky for thirty-two of his thirty-five years. As far as I know, he outlived any other horse that went with us on the wagon trip. Rocky's trail finally came to an end, but not before he could enjoy the last few years of his life having run of the ranch. Each spring he played with the new foals. Summers were spent along the creek beneath the tall cottonwood trees. I miss seeing him out in the pasture.

Figure 19. The author with her horse Rocky Fire.

Last spring, we sold the business and moved to northern California. I finally have time to work once again on my drawings. I have another horse to ride. I hope to take her to the beach this summer and ride in the surf. That's as far west as the trail will allow. Perhaps when I'm there, I'll turn east, and ride off into the sunrise. Only God knows when and where my trail will end. So now as I check my cinch and put my foot in the stirrup, I thank you, dear reader, for coming along for the ride. May all your trails be good ones, may you always ride a good horse, and if God allows, perhaps our trails will cross someday.